PELICAN BOOKS
A 244

BUTLER'S MORAL PHILOSOPHY

AUSTIN DUNCAN-JONES

Austin Duncan-Jones

BUTLER'S
MORAL PHILOSOPHY

*Here ideas never are in
themselves determinate, but become so
by the train of reasoning and the
place they stand in.*

PENGUIN BOOKS

HARMONDSWORTH · MIDDLESEX

Penguin Books Ltd, Harmondsworth, Middlesex
U.S.A.: Penguin Books Inc., 3300 Clipper Mill Road, Baltimore 11, Md
[*Educational Representative:*
D. C. Heath & Co., 285 *Columbus Avenue*, *Boston* 16, *Mass*]
AUSTRALIA: Penguin Books Pty Ltd, 200 Normanby Road,
Melbourne, S.C.5, Victoria

AGENT IN CANADA: Riverside Books Ltd, 47 Green Street,
Saint Lambert, Montreal, P.Q.

———

Made and printed in Great Britain
by Unwin Brothers Ltd
Woking and London

———

First published 1952

CONTENTS

EDITORIAL FOREWORD	7
PREFACE	9
CHRONOLOGY OF BUTLER'S LIFE	13

CHAPTER 1 · *Butler's life and writings*

§ 1 · Life and character	15
§ 2 · Butler's style	30
§ 3 · Butler as a philosopher	35

CHAPTER 2 · *Butler's theory of human nature*

§ 1 · The meaning of the word 'nature'	41
§ 2 · The hierarchy of human nature	44
§ 3 · The passions and their objects	48
§ 4 · The distinction between self-love and the particular passions	59
§ 5 · The relation between self-love and good conduct	62

CHAPTER 3 · *Conscience and its authority*

§ 1 · Butler's assumptions: the distinction between uniformity of conscience and uniformity of duty	69
§ 2 · The meaning of 'conscience'	73
§ 3 · The meaning of 'a reason for an action'	77
§ 4 · The 'intrinsic stringency' of moral qualities	85
§ 5 · Criticism of the principle of intrinsic stringency	88
§ 6 · Uniformity of conscience and uniformity of duty restated	91

CHAPTER 4 · *Selfishness and egoism*

§ 1 · Psychological egoism	95
§ 2 · The meaning of 'interested action'	105
§ 3 · Butler on Hobbes	108
§ 4 · Self-love and benevolence	112
§ 5 · Egoism in Butler's teaching	113

[5]

CONTENTS

CHAPTER 5 · *The content of morality*
§ 1 · General rules not required … 116
§ 2 · The limits of benevolence … 117
§ 3 · Butler's alternative to utilitarianism … 122

CHAPTER 6 · *Desert*
§ 1 · Butler's assumptions … 127
§ 2 · The meaning of 'freedom' and 'necessity' … 128
§ 3 · Determinism and indeterminism … 133
§ 4 · The utilitarian theory of desert … 136

CHAPTER 7 · *The place of God in Butler's ethics*
§ 1 · Butler's characteristic ethical teaching non-theological … 142
§ 2 · Final causes … 145
§ 3 · The goodness of human nature … 148
§ 4 · The love of God … 151

CHAPTER 8 · *Some ultimate problems of ethics*
§ 1 · The idea of obligation … 159
§ 2 · Naturalistic and non-naturalistic ethics … 162
§ 3 · What is a moral judgement? … 167
§ 4 · Man's aptitude for virtue … 178
§ 5 · The general questions of ethical theory … 182

INDEX … 190

EDITORIAL FOREWORD

Professor A. E. Duncan-Jones's book on the philosophy of Bishop Butler is one of a series of philosophical works which are appearing in a similar form. The series mainly consists in original studies of the work of a number of outstanding philosophers, but besides these contributions to the history of philosophy, it is also to include books on more general topics, such as logic, the theory of knowledge, political philosophy, ethics, and the philosophy of science.

The series is not designed to reflect the standpoint, or to advance the views of any one philosophical school. Since it is addressed to an audience of non-specialists as well as professional philosophers, the contributors to it have been asked to write in as untechnical a manner as their subjects allow, but they have not been expected to achieve simplicity at the cost of accuracy or completeness.

In this respect Professor Duncan-Jones has had the advantage that Butler's own style is pleasantly free from technical jargon. As a moral philosopher he wrote about subjects of general interest with the clear intention of being generally understood. But, as Professor Duncan-Jones is able to show, this plainness of Butler's language can be deceptive; for it serves to express a remarkable subtlety of thought.

A. J. AYER

PREFACE

THE purpose of this book is to expound and criticise Joseph Butler's ethical doctrines, and to pursue further some of the questions Butler raised. In this last respect I have allowed myself a good deal of freedom to expatiate, though Butler's ideas always remain in sight: but a critic might justly remark that in certain places I offer a Butlerian study in ethics rather than a study of Butler's ethics.

I have not sought to tone down the difficulties of the logical and metaphysical questions into which Butler enters, and of those which present themselves when his thoughts are dissected. But I hope that, following Butler's example, I have avoided recondite and technical forms of expression, and unexplained allusions to philosophical theories. Readers who are prepared for some degree of effort will, if my design has succeeded, find in this book not only an introduction to Butler's views, but a good deal of what might be looked for in a general introduction to ethics. That, they may be warned, is not quite the same thing as an introduction to morals or casuistry: there is little to be found here, as there is little to be found in Butler except implicitly and by way of illustration, about the constituents of a good life, there is no listing of duties, or application of moral rules to perplexing situations. But there is much discussion of the general nature of our knowledge of what is right or good, or our beliefs about it; and of the nature of that which, in those cases, is known or believed. In other words this book is chiefly concerned, as Butler in the most celebrated parts of his ethical writings was chiefly concerned, with fundamental questions about the logical status of our moral judgements in general, and not very much with the making or justifying or applying of specific moral judgements.

Butler's chief work in moral philosophy is *Fifteen sermons*

PREFACE

preached at the Rolls Chapel, first published in 1726, and supplemented in 1729 by the preface to the second edition. Next in importance is *Dissertation 2, Of the nature of virtue*, an appendix to the *Analogy of religion*, which was first published in 1736. The main purpose of the *Analogy* is to defend the Christian religion, both as known by natural reason and as revealed, against the deists. But it also contains many scattered passages which throw light on Butler's ethical doctrine.

The best edition of Butler's works is J. H. Bernard's, published in two volumes by Macmillan and Co. Ltd in 1900. There is also an edition by W. E. Gladstone, published by the Clarendon Press in 1896. Butler's minor writings are given a little more fully by Bernard than by Gladstone. Gladstone's text is, none the less, perfectly adequate for most purposes: but the editorial matter is somewhat intrusive. An edition of the *Fifteen sermons* and the *Dissertation on virtue*, by W. R. Matthews, was republished by G. Bell and Sons Ltd in 1949. In earlier generations Butler's works were frequently reprinted. Old editions are probably to be found in many libraries, and may be expected to give adequate texts of such works as they contain. Readers with access to libraries need therefore fear no greater hindrance than a little dust in seeking Butler's own words.

Throughout the present work, Butler's writings are referred to by the numbered paragraphs of Bernard's edition. The paragraphs are also numbered in Matthews' edition, and the numbering coincides almost exactly with Bernard's. Titles and references are abbreviated as follows.

Fifteen sermons are referred to as	S.
The *Preface* to the *Fifteen sermons* is referred to as	Pr.
The *Dissertation on virtue* is referred to as	D. on V.
The *Analogy of religion* is referred to as	An.
Six sermons preached upon public occasions are referred to as	S.P.

In references to the *Preface* and *Dissertation*, only one number is given, namely the paragraph number. When there are

[10]

PREFACE

two or more numbers, the last is the paragraph number, and the preceding number is that of the chapter or sermon. References to the *Analogy* contain three numbers, standing for part, chapter, and paragraph. Thus, '*S*. 2.6' will mean *Fifteen sermons*, Sermon 2, paragraph 6: '*An*. 2.8.11' will mean *Analogy* part 2, chapter 8, paragraph 11 – and so on. Butler's footnotes are referred to as 'fn.'.

Throughout this book, double inverted commas indicate quotations *verbatim* from Butler or from some other writer, or pieces of typical Butlerian phraseology. For any other purpose, single inverted commas are used. The punctuation of quotations from Butler is my own.

An excellent short study of Butler's ethics is contained in C. D. Broad's *Five types of ethical theory* (Kegan Paul, 1930). This will be referred to as '*Five types*'.

Birmingham, September 1951

CHRONOLOGY OF BUTLER'S LIFE

1692   18 May, born at Wantage in Berkshire.
1713   4 November, first letter to Clarke.
1714-15 17 March, entered commoner, Oriel College, Oxford, after some years at Mr Jones' academy at Tewkesbury.
1718   11 October, B.A.
       25 October, ordained deacon by Bishop of Salisbury, and two months later priest.
       End of the same year, appointed preacher at the Rolls Chapel.
1720   Death of Butler's friend Edward Talbot.
1722   Rector of Haughton le Skerne, near Darlington.
1725   Rector of Stanhope in Weardale (resigned Haughton).
1726   First publication of *Fifteen sermons*. Resigned the preachership of the Rolls.
1729   Second edition of *Fifteen sermons*, with preface added.
1733   Chaplain to Lord Chancellor Talbot.
1736   Clerk of the Closet to Queen Caroline.
       Prebendary of Rochester.
       First publication of *Analogy*.
1737   20 November, death of Queen Caroline.
1738   Bishop of Bristol: consecrated 3 December.
1740   Dean of St Paul's. Resigned Stanhope rectory and Rochester prebend.
1746   Clerk of the Closet to George II.
1750   Bishop of Durham.
1751   *Charge* at the primary visitation of diocese of Durham.
1752   16 June, died at Bath. 20 June, buried in Bristol Cathedral.

(The foregoing dates are Old Style. In New Style, Butler was born on 29 May 1692 and died on 27 June 1752. In modern reckoning, the year of his admission at Oriel was 1715.)

CHAPTER 1

BUTLER'S LIFE AND WRITINGS

§ 1 · *Life and character*

THE person of Butler eludes enquiry. The exterior facts of his parentage, education, and public career are well enough ascertained. But of the occupations of his daily life, or the face he showed to his friends, we have scarcely a glimpse. We are teased by the knowledge that he left a box of private papers which was ordered to be destroyed after his death, and that the order was faithfully obeyed. The standard life, the *Memoirs of the life, character, and writings of Joseph Butler* which the Rev. Thomas Bartlett published in 1839, is a remarkable instance of the art of expanding a few grains of fact into a large but unnourishing loaf.

Joseph Butler was born on 18 May 1692, at the market town of Wantage, in Berkshire, the birthplace also of King Alfred. He was the eighth and youngest child of a prosperous retired draper, whose family was rising in the world. Butler began his education at the town grammar school of Wantage, later known, with more piety than history, by the name of King Alfred's School. His family were Presbyterians, and with a view to his entering the Presbyterian ministry Butler was sent from the school at Wantage to a dissenting academy – one of a number of private institutions which offered dissenters from the established church the equivalent of a university education. This academy was kept by Mr Samuel Jones, first at Gloucester and later at Tewkesbury. We have no exact dates for Butler's earlier education, but he seems to have remained at Mr Jones' academy until early in 1715, that is, until he was nearly twenty-three. Among his fellow pupils were a number who later became distinguished men, including several who, like Butler himself, came to be reconciled to the Church of England. Of these last, the most notable, and the closest friend of Butler, was Thomas Secker, afterwards Archbishop of Canterbury. Towards the end of the time he spent at Tewkesbury, Butler entered into his celebrated correspondence with Dr Samuel Clarke. This author, best known for his *Demonstration of the being and attributes of God*, was the most eminent philosophical theologian of his time. In his writings Butler had sought the rational confirmation of Christian doctrine to which a large part of his own work was to be devoted. He addressed Clarke with great modesty, and in the earlier letters anonymously; but without any compromise of intellectual independence. The correspondence as it has survived extended over about four years. Clarke entered with great good will and cordiality into the objections to his own *a priori* arguments for the existence and nature of God laid before him by an unknown young man, and complimented Butler, very justly, on the philosophical penetration and freedom from controversial bitterness displayed in his conduct of the debate.

At the time when the Clarke correspondence began, Butler's mind must already have been turning towards the Church of England. On 17 March 1715 he was entered as a commoner at Oriel College, Oxford, with the intention of preparing himself for holy orders. There is no evidence that Butler had any money cares at this time of his life, and it may be supposed that he remained on good terms with his family, and that his father was ready to make him an allowance, in spite of his having forsaken Presbyterianism. At Oxford he formed a close friendship with another undergraduate, Edward Talbot, the second son of William Talbot, Bishop of Salisbury, and later of Durham. Edward Talbot died as a young man in 1720, but the Talbot family continued to be Butler's firm friends, and it was their patronage which smoothed his early career in the church.

Butler was discontented with what he regarded as the pedantic technicalities of his philosophical and theological

§ 1 · LIFE AND CHARACTER

studies at Oxford; "our people here", he wrote (Letters to Clarke, 7.5), "never had any doubt in their lives concerning a received opinion; so that I cannot mention a difficulty to them". He consulted Clarke about his studies, and about a project of migrating to Cambridge, which unhappily came to nothing. On 11 October 1718 he took his first degree at Oxford, and soon afterwards he was ordained deacon, and a little later priest, by the Bishop of Salisbury. Immediately afterwards he was appointed Preacher at the Rolls Chapel. The stipend was small, and we find that his family seem to have continued to supply him with funds. In 1722, William Talbot, then Bishop of Durham, made him Rector of Haughton le Skerne, near Darlington; and the same patron transferred him, in 1725, to the richly endowed rectory of Stanhope in Weardale. In 1726 Butler published the *Fifteen sermons*, which are to be the principal source of the topics discussed in the following chapters, and in the same year he resigned the preachership of the Rolls.

For the next seven years he lived at his rectory of Stanhope in complete retirement from the worlds both of learning and of fashion – Butler's career suggests that they were not so sharply divided from one another as modern people might suppose. In 1732 Queen Caroline, whose lively and enquiring mind was later the cause of an abrupt change of scene in Butler's life, asked Archbishop Blackburne whether Dr Butler was not dead: the Archbishop replied "not dead, ma'am, but buried". But the time of retirement was not wasted: apart from the duties of a parish priest, his principal occupation during those seven years must have been the writing of the *Analogy of religion, natural and revealed, to the constitution and course of nature*. It was on this work, rather than the *Sermons*, that Butler's reputation chiefly rested during the century or so which followed its publication in 1736.

In 1733 Lord Chancellor Talbot, the elder brother of Butler's friend Edward, drew Butler from his retirement by appointing him to be his chaplain. Butler's earlier friend, Secker, was now a chaplain to the King: through him Butler was again brought to the notice of Queen Caroline, who in 1736 appointed him her Clerk of the Closet. In the same year the Lord Chancellor presented him to a prebend of Rochester Cathedral. In his attendance upon the Queen, Butler's chief duty was to make one each evening, between seven and nine, at the gatherings of men of wit and learning which the Queen was fond of assembling.

It was at the time of Butler's employment in Queen Caroline's service that he met John Byrom, who left several pages describing their conversation at Dr Hartley's house (*Remains* of John Byrom, Vol. 2, Pt. 1, 28 March 1737). Unhappily Byrom has given us a clearer view of his own mind than of Butler's. "The Dr. [Butler] talked with much mildness", Byrom says, "and myself with too much impetuosity." The talk turned first upon Byrom's shorthand system, which he was hoping to impart to the young Duke of Cumberland, third son of the King and Queen, then a boy of about sixteen. Butler told an anecdote of the Queen and her son. "He told us of the Duke's forwardness, of his passing by when he (the Dr.) was reading Hobbes to a certain person [the Queen], and that certain person saying, Well, and what do you think of this? And the Duke said that there must be right and wrong before human laws, which supposed right and wrong; and besides, wherever was there that state of nature that he talked of? who ever lived in it? And that person ... Well, but if you was left to yourself, what would you do? And the Duke said, I cannot tell what pleasure, &c., might do to blind me, but unless it did, so and so, &c." Butler's admirers will wish to believe that one who wrote so incisively cannot have spoken so lamely, and will conjecture that the story as told by Butler had a nicer edge: but it is upon such scraps that they are reduced to feed. From Hobbes the conversation passed to Newton, Pascal, and Christian evidences: Butler defending at all points the use of reason, and Byrom making large claims for prophecy, miracles, and authority. Byrom, like Wesley in a later record of a conversation with Butler, gives his own

§ 1 · LIFE AND CHARACTER

arguments a good deal more fully than Butler's. Butler evidently drew the attention of the enthusiastic Byrom to the fact that the word 'authority' has many senses, that there are good and bad forms of authority, and that the respect due to them depends much on circumstances. But his quiet voice is scarcely heard. We surmise that for each of Byrom's generalisations he could offer an exception. "I considered a man", says Byrom, "how he was born under the parental authority, that if a person should invite a child to leave his father's house, he might give very good reasons, as that he should fare better, have finer things, &c., but still the child would stick to the parental authority." "But how would you do", said Butler, "if your father commanded what was contrary to the laws of God?" Byrom seems to have admitted and denied the objection in one breath, and passed on to military discipline and Abraham. "Dr. B. mentioned Mahomet", who was then enlisted on the side of authority by Byrom. "But would it not have been better", said Butler, "if the people had followed Mahomet in what was right, and distinguished the wrong from it?" After Butler had left, Byrom said "I wished I had Dr. Butler's temper and calmness, yet not quite, because I thought he was a little too little vigorous".

During the short time which intervened before the Queen's death, on 20 November 1737, Butler won her respect and liking to such a degree that she spoke of him, and according to one witness of him alone, on her deathbed, and desired that he should be given preferment.

Preferment came in the following year, but in the somewhat disappointing shape of the bishopric of Bristol, the poorest see in England. In Butler's letter of acceptance to Sir Robert Walpole – among many expressions of gratitude – he wrote "indeed the bishoprick of Bristol is not very suitable either to the condition of my fortune, or the circumstances of my preferment; nor, as I should have thought, answerable to the recommendation with which I was honoured. But you will excuse me, sir, if I think of this last with greater sensibility than the conduct of affairs will admit of". This letter seems to embarrass Bernard, who describes it as "one of the curiosities of literature". There is no reason for Butler's admirers to be disconcerted by it, if causes and circumstances are fairly considered. Butler knew that, to discharge the office of a bishop, in church and state, as the eighteenth century conceived its duties, he would be obliged, however modest his own tastes might be, to keep up a town house and a country house, to travel frequently between London and his diocese, as well as about the diocese, to admit company to his table, and to attend from time to time at Court and in the House of Lords. Even with the strictest economy, such a train of living could not be furnished from the revenue of about £400 a year which was all that at that time belonged to the see of Bristol. It followed that, as Bishop of Bristol, he would be compelled to hold other benefices *in commendam*, if he was to command an adequate income. He could readily obtain leave to do so, and church pluralities were not then thought discreditable. It is clear that Butler disliked the practice, at any rate as far as parochial cures were concerned: when he became chaplain to the Lord Chancellor he stipulated that he should be free to spend half the year at Stanhope, and we have evidence of his reluctance, later, to give leave of absence to parish incumbents in his own diocese.

Early in 1740, not long after his acceptance of the bishopric of Bristol, Butler was presented to the deanery of St Paul's. He then resigned the rectory of Stanhope and his prebend at Rochester, which he would no doubt have been free to keep. The resignation of the Rochester prebend is particularly significant, because the duties of residence are likely to have been very small, and only a man of unusually scrupulous mind would have felt any difficulty about retaining it. As Dean of St Paul's he would be able to combine his duties at the cathedral with the attendances at Court and in Parliament which brought him to London as a matter of course; and he would know that in his absence there was an adequate establishment of clergy for the service of the cathedral.

The well-known meeting between Butler and John Wesley

§ 1 · LIFE AND CHARACTER

took place in 1739, and was minuted afterwards by Wesley. The record of it is to be found in Gladstone's edition of Butler's works, but not in Bernard's. Wesley and his followers had then just begun to infringe church order by preaching and ministering without due diocesan authority. Butler, as Bishop of Bristol, expected Wesley, as a priest of the Church of England, to conform to that church's discipline, and made the mistake of reasoning with a man who believed himself to be directly inspired. It is unfortunate that one sentence of Butler's, often quoted, inevitably comes before a modern reader with an air of slang. When Butler said, as reported by Wesley, "Sir, the pretending to extraordinary revelations and gifts of the Holy Ghost is a horrid thing, a very horrid thing", he meant, of course, that it was a thing which shocked and horrified. Wesley's reply was that he pretended to no such revelations "but what every Christian may receive". His last address to the Bishop makes it clear, however, that such revelations as every Christian might receive were often to be expected to conflict with the diocesan system. Having taken his stand, Wesley brings down the curtain on a dialogue in which the Bishop's speaking part is rather less than half the length of his own. As Gladstone charitably remarks, "it is extremely difficult for one of the parties to a conversation to recollect in full the words of the other".

For the last dozen years of Butler's life we have very few notices of his occupations, apart from the official record of his appointments. He published no substantial work after the *Analogy*. That his intellectual vigour did not decline will be shown later. One tantalising glimpse of the meditations which occupied him has not been too often quoted to appear again. The following note is by Dr Josiah Tucker, later Dean of Gloucester, who was Butler's domestic chaplain at Bristol. (I omit Dr Tucker's part in the conversation). "The late Dr Butler ... had a singular notion respecting large communities and public bodies. ... His custom was, when at Bristol, to walk for hours in his garden, in the darkest night which the time of the year could afford, and I had frequently

[21]

CH. 1 · LIFE AND WRITINGS

the honour to attend him. After walking some time he would stop suddenly and ask the question: 'What security is there against the insanity of individuals? The physicians know of none; and as to divines, we have no data either from Scripture or from reason to go upon relative to this affair.' ... He would then take another turn, and again stop short: 'Why might not whole communities and public bodies be seized with fits of insanity, as well as individuals?' ... 'Nothing but this principle, that they are liable to insanity equally at least with private persons, can account for the major part of those transactions of which we read in history.'"

In 1746 Butler was made Clerk of the Closet to the King, but there is no evidence, nor is it probable, that this appointment brought him into the same intimacy with the King as he had enjoyed with the late Queen during his earlier clerkship. There is an ill authenticated story that in 1747 he refused the archbishopric of Canterbury, saying that "it was too late for him to try to support a falling Church". The remark is out of character: Butler would not have supposed that the ill prospects of the Church, as seen with the world's eyes, released him from his duties towards it, or annulled the divine promises which had been made to it. But the story may have borrowed credit from a famous passage in the *Advertisement* prefixed to the *Analogy*. "It is come, I know not how, to be taken for granted by many persons that Christianity is not so much as a subject of enquiry; but that it is now at length discovered to be fictitious. And accordingly they treat it as if in the present age this were an agreed point among all people of discernment; and nothing remained but to set it up as a principal subject of mirth and ridicule, as it were by way of reprisals for its having so long interrupted the pleasures of the world." The disillusioned tone is characteristic, and the wit cannot be the wit of gaiety.

The offer of the bishopric of Durham, with which Butler's name is most often associated, came in 1750; it came under such ungrateful conditions that Butler was very near to refusing. The Duke of Newcastle was then the leading minister.

§ 1 · LIFE AND CHARACTER

The story is told that the Duke intended, on Butler's translation, to separate from the palatine bishopric the lieutenancy of the county, which had been annexed to it. If the story is true, Butler would certainly have been sincere in the comment he is reported to have made: "it was a matter of indifference to him", he said, "whether he died Bishop of Bristol or of Durham; but that it was not a matter of indifference to him whether or not the honours of the see were invaded during his incumbency; and he therefore begged to be allowed to continue Bishop of Bristol." To most people today the annexing of civil authority to ecclesiastical will seem improper, and the lustre which might have been withdrawn from the great palatine see in favour of some rising lord hardly worth regarding. But to Butler the withdrawal of the lieutenancy would have appeared as a step in the process of diminishing the Church establishment: that he would have held it a duty to defend the establishment against encroachment may be seen from the hints of a general view of Church and State which he gives in *S.P. 5*.

On another impediment to Butler's acceptance we have the evidence of Butler's long letter to the Duke of Newcastle, dated at Bristol, 5 August 1750 (in Gladstone, but not in Bernard). The Duke wished that a prebend of Durham should be given to a certain Dr Thomas Chapman, and a story was current that Chapman was to have the first prebend vacant after Butler's translation. Had Butler given any promise, in advance of preferment, even a tacit promise, by which he would have been bound afterwards in the exercise of a new office, he would have committed the grave offence of simony — though, in the then state of church law it is not to be supposed that he would have been called to account for it. The polite and submissive language of the letter does not conceal Butler's firm intention not to accept the see unless upon his own conditions — that is, upon none. "Your grace will please to remember", he wrote, "that when you mentioned this to me near three quarters of a year ago I made not a word of answer, but went on talking of other things, and upon your repeating the mention of it at the same time, just as I was going out of your dressing room, I told your Grace it did not admit of an answer. This my silence, and this my reply, were owing to my being in so great a surprise at such a thing being asked of me *beforehand* that I durst not trust myself to talk upon the subject. But upon settling within myself what I ought to say I proposed to wait upon your Grace and let you know that I could not take any church promotion upon the condition of any such promise or intimation as your Grace seemed to expect." He goes on to say that, even having made it plain to the Duke that there was no promise, he would not think it possible to prefer Dr Chapman, since "this affair that I am to give Dr Chapman the first prebend of Durham is common talk at Cambridge" (where Chapman was master of Magdalene College): he must therefore pass over Chapman, since if he did otherwise the world would certainly assume that a simoniac promise had been given. He closes with a postscript, reminding the poor bewildered Duke of the probability that a prebend of Durham will fall into the hands of the Crown, which might bestow it on Chapman without the Bishop being concerned.

(The foregoing summary of the incident seems to be what follows from the terms of Butler's letter. A more complicated and less intelligible account of it is given by Bartlett and the *Dictionary of national biography*.)

The letter was evidently effective, for Butler's formal election to the see followed a month later. Ties at Bristol and in Parliament prevented him from establishing himself at Durham until June 1751. In answer to the congratulations of a friend, he wrote "I foresee many difficulties in the station I am coming into, and no advantage worth thinking of, except some greater power of being serviceable to others. ... It would be a melancholy thing in the close of life to have no reflections to entertain one's self with, but that one had spent the revenues of the bishoprick of Durham in a sumptuous course of living, and enriched one's friends with the promotions of it, instead of having really set one's self to do good and promote worthy men: yet this right use of fortune and

§ 1 · LIFE AND CHARACTER

power is more difficult than the generality of even good people think, and requires both a guard upon one's self, and a strength of mind to withstand solicitations, greater, I wish I may not find it, than I am master of."

Although he was only effectively Bishop of Durham for about a year, his new diocese was the occasion of Butler's last published work, the *Charge delivered to the clergy*, at the primary visitation of the diocese of Durham, 1751. The Durham *Charge* is of the greatest interest to those who wish to know more of the condition of the Church in the eighteenth century. It is too little connected with the main subject of this book to be analysed here in detail. Butler's topic is the pastoral office of the clergy, with particular reference to "external religion". By its comprehensive review of the life of a parish priest and his parishioners, by its judicious distinctions and qualifications, and perhaps not least by the typical references to the littleness of what human efforts can achieve, the *Charge* demonstrates that the depth and nicety of Butler's mind were unimpaired to the end of his life. Horace Walpole remarked that "the Bishop of Durham had been wafted to that see in a cloud of metaphysics, and remained absorbed in it". Probably Walpole had no better foundation for his *bon mot* than the fact that Butler had published a metaphysical work fifteen years before, and that he was not in the habit of making political speeches. The Durham *Charge* illustrates, both that the intellectual powers which produced the *Analogy* were as active as ever, and that metaphysics was not, as Walpole chose to fancy, their sole preoccupation.

Within a few months, Butler's health broke down. On medical advice he removed, first to Clifton, and then to Bath. But it must have been clear to him and to those around him that he was a dying man. After some weeks of great weakness he died at Bath on 16 June 1752, aged sixty. He was attended during his last illness by his chaplain, Dr Nathaniel Forster. A number of Forster's letters of this time survive. He describes Butler's symptoms in more detail than modern readers will desire to hear, but tells us little of Butler's words and thoughts. From another correspondent we know that during the last few days Butler was almost unconscious. Forster was warmly devoted to the Bishop: writing in great distress and agitation, he probably did not feel capable of producing anything beyond the essential medical bulletins. To his grief for Butler were added anxieties about the office of executor, with which Butler charged him five days before his death: Forster was unversed in the business, and feared that he would be called on for disbursements which he had no means of making. Bishop Benson, of Gloucester, who was with Butler shortly before his death, describes their last meeting very briefly. "The last time I went in to the bishop, I found both his understanding and speech, after a little sleep he had had, more perfect than they were before. This made my taking leave so much the more painful. It must be, as he with a good deal of emotion said, a 'farewell for ever', and said kind and affecting things more than I could bear."

Butler was buried in Bristol Cathedral on 20 June 1752. The place is marked now by a tarnished brass plate in the wall. Elsewhere in the Cathedral is a marble monument, erected in 1834, with a long English inscription, the work of Robert Southey.

Butler never married. He was of a reserved and somewhat melancholy disposition, and if we are to believe Byrom was diffident in conversation: though it is hard to suppose that conversational evasions would have satisfied the vigorous curiosity of Queen Caroline. His quiet and unworldly cast of mind did not prevent him from winning the devotion of friends. Through his undergraduate acquaintance with Edward Talbot the whole of Talbot's family became attached to him: and throughout his life he is spoken of with affectionate warmth, though with sadly little detail, by those who knew him best. The Talbot family was influential, and could and did forward Butler's career in the church: but a man with so few showy qualities as Butler possessed cannot have had the power, even if he had had the will, to cultivate friendships from ambitious views.

§ 1 · LIFE AND CHARACTER

Two details of Butler's character appear from a number of hints: his attitude to money, and his love of improving and restoring buildings. It may be surmised that Butler did not find it possible to think about money for very long at a time, and in consequence was not what is called businesslike. The two small account books in his hand which are preserved at Oriel College give the impression of a man who made resolutions of better management from time to time, and whose resolution tended to flag. Among the shadowy traces of the Stanhope period is the story told eighty years later by an aged parishioner of "Rector Butler". "He lived very retired", said the old man, and "was very kind": and (here, I suspect, the old man's words begin to be paraphrased) he "could not resist the importunities of common beggars, who, knowing his infirmity, pursued him so earnestly as sometimes to drive him back into his house as his only escape." When we remember the following passage from one of Butler's charity sermons (*S.P.* 2.14) — "others make a custom of giving to idle vagabonds: a kind of charity, very improperly so called, which one really wonders people can allow themselves in, merely to be relieved from importunity, or at best to gratify a false good nature" — we understand the conflict between conscience and kindness to which the beggars of Stanhope condemned their poor rector: and we almost begin to believe that it was on their account that Rector Butler rode his black pony, and "rode always very fast".

A later story describes an appeal to Butler for a Durham charity. Butler sent for his steward, to know what money he had in hand. The answer was "Five hundred pounds, my lord". "Five hundred pounds!" exclaimed Butler, "what a shame for a bishop to have so much money! Give it all to this gentleman for his charitable plan." Both the gift and the vagueness as to his resources are characteristic of Butler.

It will be seen that a curious fact about the estate which Butler bequeathed must be attributed to luck rather than good management. "I should feel ashamed of myself", Butler remarked once to his secretary, "if I could leave ten thousand

[27]

pounds behind me." When his property came to be disposed of, it amounted to a little over £9000. This was a much smaller fortune than might have been left by a man of frugal habits who had held valuable preferments for nearly thirty years, as well as having inherited something from his father. By Butler's will, all that he left was divided into a number of small legacies, distributed over kinsfolk, friends, servants, the Newcastle infirmary, and the Society for the Propagation of the Gospel.

There were two causes of the relative smallness of Butler's estate. One was his readiness, already illustrated, to give large sums away. The other was his passion for building and improving. So far as can be judged, Butler's building projects had as a rule no close connection with his own need for a residence: it was rather that he could not bear to see a building for which he was responsible in bad order. The first instance was at his rectory of Haughton le Skerne, which was almost in ruins. Butler released his predecessor on easy terms from his obligation to make good dilapidations, and set about producing a house from a ruin. His friends feared that the enterprise would swallow up the small income he had at the time: and it has been suggested that Secker's hope of delivering Butler from the building scheme had something to do with Bishop Talbot's gift of the Stanhope living, with its large income and solid rectory house.

As Bishop of Bristol Butler was again saddled with a dilapidated house. He reconstructed the whole interior of the palace, at a cost which is said to have been about equal to the income of the see throughout his tenure, using also a large quantity of cedar wood which the merchants of the town presented to him. The Bristol work included the reconstruction of the palace chapel, where he erected over the altar a white marble cross, inlaid in a slab of black marble. In the East window over it was "a small crucifix with the B. Virgin and St John under the cross weeping, of old glass". This act, commonplace today, was at that period thought extraordinary in a bishop of the reformed Church. It was combined with the

§ 1 · LIFE AND CHARACTER

Durham *Charge* to form the raw material of a legend, fabricated some time after his death, that Butler secretly adhered to the Church of Rome. The invention would not have greatly surprised the author of the sermon *Upon the government of the tongue*. The whole of this sermon repays the reader, but we can only afford space for a small specimen. "The thing here ... referred to is talkativeness: a disposition to be talking, abstracted from the consideration of what is to be said; with very little or no regard to, or thought of doing, either good or harm ... And if these people expect to be heard and regarded – for there are some content merely with talking – they will invent to engage your attention: and when they have heard the least imperfect hint of an affair, they will out of their own head add the circumstances of time and place, and other matters to make out their story and give the appearance of probability to it: not that they have any concern about being believed otherwise than as a means of being heard. ... The tongue used in such a licentious manner is like a sword in the hands of a madman" (*S.* 4.3, and 5).

As Bishop of Durham, Butler began improvements at Auckland, and reconstructed large parts of Durham Castle. During the later years of his life he had a house at Hampstead, which he used instead of a town house. Here he put up a number of painted glass windows, illustrating scripture subjects, in which some pieces of sixteenth-century glass were incorporated – the talkative people who have just been mentioned concluded that they were a present from the Pope. In spite of the sombre light which these windows may suggest, the Hampstead house is described by one of the Talbot ladies, who were frequent visitors, as "a most enchanting, gay, pretty, elegant house". It is here alone that we imagine Butler fitting up a house for himself, and for quiet social pleasures.

I have tried to piece together such oddments as I can of the external circumstances which form the staple of most biographies. That I have had to lean somewhat heavily on trivialities, and that the material with which Boswell would have delighted us is so scarce, is perhaps not altogether an accident. The portrait by which Butler is to be judged is the portrait of his mind. He has left us his own record of a fuller life than he could find in houses, or church government, or charitable schemes, or polite conversation. It is perhaps communicated to us most freely in his less strictly philosophical sermons – the sermon on talkativeness already quoted; the sermons on compassion, self-deceit, the love of God, and the ignorance of man; and in parts of the *Sermons on Public Occasions*.

The reader will perceive that the whole interest of Butler's personality lies in his character as a minister and doctor of the Christian Church. Those who not only reject or doubt the Church's doctrines, but – what does not necessarily follow – also dislike and condemn the Church as a society, and the lives of its members, may have concluded already that the work of such a man as has been described cannot engage their thoughts. I venture to advertise such readers that in the pages which follow they need fear no nauseating excesses of unction and sanctimony. In his philosophical writings Butler asks for no concessions: as much as the most secular philosopher, he appeals to common sense, refined by whatever nice qualifications and rigorous analyses we are able to command. It is, I fear, those who hope for edification who may be disappointed in the Butler now to be put before them.

§ 2 · *Butler's style*

BUTLER's manner of writing was consciously formed. There are several passages in which he states clearly enough the principles to which he means to adhere. The first which stands out is that precision is to be preferred to ease and elegance. "It is very unallowable for a work of imagination or entertainment not to be of easy comprehension, but may be unavoidable in a work of another kind, where a man is not to form or accommodate, but to state things as he finds them" (*Pr.* 6). There are two causes which may make a treatise

§ 2 · BUTLER'S STYLE

obscure and hard to follow: the inherent difficulties of the subject – for "everything is not to be understood with the same ease that some things are"; and "confusion and perplexity", that is, heedless and slipshod thought and expression (*Pr.* 8). A writer is not open to criticism unless he is obscure from the second cause. Whether an abstruse manner of writing can be avoided is only to be judged by those who take the trouble to follow the argument, and to find out "how far the things insisted upon, *and not other things*, might have been put in a plainer manner" (*Pr.* 7 – my italics). A writer who aims at easy reading at any price may be constrained to substitute "other things" for the question he is supposed to be treating.

Secondly, Butler had certain clearly held opinions about the functioning of language. Of the meanings of words he took what it is now fashionable to call a 'contextual' view: he held, that is, that words are not, as too great reliance on concise dictionaries might make us suppose, bricks or atoms of meaning, each of which enters without change of shape size or mass into walls or molecules of meaning, whose properties can be deduced from those of their components. To amplify Butler a little, language operates in wholes of varying size and complexity, whose ingredients include people's thoughts, acts, and situations, as well as their words: and the whole contributes as much to the force of the word or idiom as the word to that of the whole. "I must desire the reader not to take any assertion alone by itself, but to consider the whole of what is said upon it: because this is necessary, not only in order to judge of the truth of it, but often, such is the nature of language, to see the very meaning of the assertion" (*Pr.* 32). Thus, although as we shall see Butler adopted from Locke the notion of the imperfection of language, he did not follow Locke in supposing that a few simple maxims of definition would provide a remedy.

Thirdly, then, "language is in its very nature inadequate, ambiguous, liable to infinite abuse, even from negligence" (that is, without intent to deceive: *An.* 2.3.8). Words do not come to our ears and lips with clear and distinct meanings ready made. Many errors may be avoided by drawing explicit distinctions between the senses of a word. Butler illustrates the need for distinctions in his treatment of the theory of universal selfishness (*Pr.* 35 and elsewhere), which is to be considered in chapter 4. One of the commonest of such errors is the habit – breeder of many insidious philosophical theories – of tacitly using a common word in an uncommon sense, or in both its common and its innovated sense indiscriminately. "Suppose a man of learning to be writing a grave book upon human nature: ... amongst other things the following one would require to be accounted for: the appearance of benevolence ... in men towards each other ... Cautious of being deceived with outward show, he retires within himself to see exactly what that is in the mind of man from whence this appearance proceeds; and, upon deep reflection, asserts the principle ... to be only the love of power, and delight in the exercise of it. Would not every body think here was a mistake of one word for another?" (*S.* 1.6, fn.). Here is another passage on a connected theme. "If, because every particular affection is a man's own, and the pleasure arising from its gratification his own pleasure, ... such particular affection must be called self-love, according to this way of speaking no creature whatever can possibly act but merely from self-love ... But then *this is not the language of mankind:* or, if it were, we should want words to express the difference between the principle of an action proceeding from cool consideration that it will be to my own advantage, and an action, suppose of revenge or of friendship, by which a man runs upon certain ruin to do evil or good to another" (*S.* 11.7 – my italics). If the advocates of philosophical paradoxes paused to ask themselves 'is this the language of mankind?' the intellectual scene would be duller, certainly, but saner.

Taking these views of the nature, and the use and abuse, of language, Butler was led to cultivate a style which is not smooth or easy, but remarkably exact, economical, and searching. It is unrelieved by the neatly turned phrases with

§ 2 · BUTLER'S STYLE

which Berkeley entertains the reader, or the satirical sallies to which Hume was sometimes willing to sacrifice precision. A famous historian was said to write in a style in which it is impossible to tell the truth: it would not be a great exaggeration to say that in Butler's style it is impossible to tell lies. The dangers, both of rash overstatement, and of allowing misunderstanding to arise from thoughtlessly chosen expressions, were always in Butler's mind. The result is that his sentences strike many readers as heavy and cumbersome: they are sometimes built up to great length, their sense shaded and modulated by conditions and relative clauses, and parenthetic exceptions and tonings down. To my mind Butler's qualifications and amplifications, and his flat unadorned diction, often have a charm of their own. I subjoin one or two specimens.

(Of the existence of sympathy between men.) "There is such a natural principle of attraction in man towards man that having trod the same tract of land, having breathed in the same climate, barely having been born in the same artificial district or division, becomes the occasion of contracting acquaintances and familiarities many years after: for anything may serve the purpose. Thus relations merely nominal are sought and invented, not by governors, but by the lowest of the people, which are found sufficient to hold mankind together in little fraternities and copartnerships: weak ties indeed, and what may afford fund enough for ridicule if they are absurdly considered as the real principles of that union, but they are in truth merely the occasions, as anything may be of anything, upon which our nature carries us on according to its own previous bent and bias, which occasions therefore would be nothing at all were there not this prior disposition and bias of nature." (*S.* 1.10.)

(Of man's incapacity for judging what would be the best of all possible worlds.) "For though it be admitted that, from the first principles of our nature, we unavoidably judge or determine some ends to be absolutely in themselves preferable to others, and that the ends now mentioned, or if they run up into one, that this one is absolutely the best, and consequently that we must conclude the ultimate end designed in the constitution of nature and conduct of Providence is the most virtue and happiness possible; yet we are far from being able to judge what particular disposition of things would be most friendly and assistant to virtue, or what means might be absolutely necessary to produce the most happiness in a system of such extent as our own world may be, taking in all that is past and to come, though we should suppose it detached from the whole of things. Indeed, we are so far from being able to judge of this that we are not judges what may be the necessary means of raising and conducting one person to the highest perfection and happiness of his nature. Nay, even in the little affairs of the present life we find men of different educations and ranks are not competent judges of the conduct of each other." (*An.* Introduction 10.)

One further passage will illustrate at the same time Butler's use of language and his sense of his own difficulties in using it. (He has been speaking of the duty of truthfulness.) "However, though veracity as well as justice is to be our rule of life, it must be added – otherwise a snare will be laid in the way of some plain men – that the use of common forms of speech, generally understood, cannot be falsehood; and, in general, that there can be no designed falsehood without designing to deceive. It must likewise be observed that, in numberless cases, a man may be under the strictest obligations to what he foresees will deceive without his intending it. For it is impossible not to foresee that the words and actions of men, in different ranks and employments and of different educations, will perpetually be mistaken by each other; and it cannot but be so whilst they will judge with the utmost carelessness, as they daily do, of what they are not, perhaps, enough informed to be competent judges of, even though they considered it with great attention." (*D. on V.* 11.)

In thought and reasoning there may be a malady of morbid scrupulosity, as much as in morals. I do not think that Butler suffered from it. But the very individual passage last cited shows that his impulse to balance and qualify came not only, as it might in any writer, from the desire to make the best of his own thoughts and not be misunderstood, but from a sense that the right use of language was as much a matter of obligation as any activity whatever.

§ 3 · *Butler as a philosopher*

BUTLER'S distinctive qualities as a moral philosopher will be sufficiently illustrated in the chapters which follow. Something may be said here of his intellectual powers in general. The *Analogy* is not, strictly speaking, a general treatise on philosophical theology, still less on metaphysics: it is a thorough and painstaking countering of objections to natural theology, and to the Christian revelation, supposed to be made from a certain point of view, namely that of the deists. Butler's aim, he explains, is to apply a certain method, namely a method of drawing probabilities from analogies, to religion "in general, both natural and revealed; taking for proved that there is an intelligent author of nature and natural governor of the world" (*An.* Introduction 8). This premiss he assumed to be admitted by his opponents. They differed from him in rejecting providential interposition in human life by the "author of nature", ties of obligation between men and their maker, and his revelation of himself through Christ and the Church which he founded. Theoretical assaults on Christianity now seldom come in that particular guise, and the *Analogy* is therefore of interest rather as a monument of Butler's intellectual qualities than for the general course of its argument.

We have enough evidence, in the *Analogy* and elsewhere, to allow us to see that Butler moved among metaphysical problems with perfect mastery. The earliest illustrations, and those furthest from the line of thought for which Butler is best known, are in the Clarke correspondence. There the empirically minded Butler shows an aptitude for *a priori* metaphysics which does not seem inferior to that of Spinoza or Leibniz: combined, of course, with the careful discriminations

CH. 1 · LIFE AND WRITINGS

of language so typical of his own later work. Unfortunately the quasi-geometrical manner of deduction which Clarke practised, and in which Butler here couches his criticisms, does not lend itself to brief quotation. The most sustained example of what Butler could do in this line is in the first letter, written when he was twenty-one. In the seventh and eighth letters he gives a statement of a difficulty in what is sometimes called the 'metaphysic of ethics' from which I subjoin an extract. The question is how, and in what sense, men can be said to be free to act virtuously – a question which will be referred to again in ch. 6. Butler has argued that "a disposition to be influenced by right motives is a *sine qua non* to virtuous actions", and continues: "Since it may be said, as you hint, that this stronger disposition to be influenced by vicious motives may have been contracted by repeated acts of wickedness, we will pitch upon the first vicious action anyone is guilty of. No man would have committed this first vicious action if he had not had a stronger (at least as strong) disposition in him to be influenced by the motives of the vicious action than by the motives of the contrary virtuous action; from whence I infallibly conclude that, since every man has committed some first vice, every man had, antecedent to the commission of it, a stronger disposition to be influenced by the vicious than the virtuous motive. My difficulty upon this is that a stronger disposition to be influenced by the vicious than the virtuous motive (which every one has antecedent to his first vice) seems ... to put the man in the same condition as though he was indifferent to the virtuous motive; and since an indifferency to the virtuous motive would have incapacitated a man from being a moral agent, or contracting guilt, is not a stronger disposition to be influenced by the vicious motive as great an incapacity?" (Letters to Clarke, 8.2.)

The first point considered in the *Analogy*, under the heading of natural religion, is human survival of death. Butler's purpose here is rather to remove difficulties than to give a proof. He carries the process further in the first *Dissertation*, *Of personal identity*, appended to the *Analogy*. This *Dissertation*

§ 3 · BUTLER AS A PHILOSOPHER

gives us another specimen of Butler's general powers as a metaphysician. He takes up the question what is meant by 'personal identity' at the point at which Locke left it. Butler has not said the last word on this perplexing question. But he makes at least one very telling point against Locke. Locke had defined personal identity in terms of "consciousness". His meaning is not altogether clear, but it seems to have been that, when we speak of two acts at different times as acts of the same person, we mean that the doer of the later act remembers, or is capable of remembering, the doing of the earlier act. Butler points out that, in this relation of remembering, the idea of personal identity is presupposed, and it would be circular to define personal identity in terms of the relation of remembering. "One should really think it self-evident that consciousness of personal identity presupposes, and therefore cannot constitute, personal identity; any more than knowledge, in any other case, can constitute truth, which it presupposes. This wonderful mistake may possibly have arisen from hence; that to be endued with consciousness is inseparable from the idea of a person . . . For this might be expressed inaccurately thus, that consciousness makes personality; and from hence it might be concluded to make personal identity. But though present consciousness of what we at present do and feel is necessary to our being the persons we now are, yet present consciousness of past actions or feelings is not necessary to our being the same persons who performed those actions or had those feelings." (*Dissertation* 1, 3–4.) Thus, even if it were not for the circularity of the memory theory, it would leave in an impersonal limbo the large number of actions which we do not and cannot remember. "To say that it [consciousness] makes personal identity, or is necessary to our being the same persons, is to say that a person has not existed a single moment, nor done one action, but what he can remember" (*Dissertation* 1, 3).

Butler's own view was that the notion of personal identity is indefinable, but that it is easy to point out how it comes to present itself to us. "When it is asked wherein personal

[37]

identity consists, the answer should be the same as if it were asked wherein consists similitude or equality; that all attempts to define would but perplex it. Yet there is no difficulty in ascertaining the idea. For as, upon two triangles being compared or viewed together, there arises to the mind the idea of similitude, or upon twice two and four the idea of equality; so likewise, upon comparing the consciousness of one's self, or one's own existence, in any two moments, there as immediately arises to the mind the idea of personal identity. And as the two former comparisons not only *give* us the ideas of similitude and equality, but also *show* us that two triangles are alike and twice two and four are equal; so the latter comparison not only *gives* us the idea of personal identity, but also *shows* us the identity of ourselves in those two moments." (*Dissertation* 1, 2 – my italics.) That is, we form or become aware of the idea of personal identity by the very same act in which we recognise instances of it.

Finally it may be worth while to illustrate a quality of a rather different kind – the shrewdness and clarity of Butler's psychological generalisations. Examples may be found throughout Butler's works. One of his most sustained passages of psychological analysis is to be found in a chapter of the *Analogy* in which he considers human life as a state of "probation" and "moral discipline". Here he discusses the nature and effects of habit. Having mentioned the familiar fact that by repetition of similar actions in similar situations habits are formed, he points out that there is an analogy between the forming of habits and the association of ideas or impressions: people who have often seen smoking fires form a habit, as it were, of thinking of fire when they see smoke. But whereas habits in the familiar sense become stronger by repetition, a purely passive repetition of the same train of thought makes a progressively weaker impression on us. The first time I notice a cigarette end smouldering on the floor, I may be greatly struck by the danger of fire: I may at that point pick up the cigarette end and extinguish it, and so take the first step in forming a habit of exercising similar vigilance against fire

§ 3 · BUTLER AS A PHILOSOPHER

on all occasions. This habit of taking active precautions will continue to operate, even though, from familiarity, my imaginative realisation of the dangers of fire becomes fainter. But if I don't take any active steps on the first occasion, the mere repetition of smouldering cigarette ends, so far from leading me to form a useful habit, will make me less likely to do so, as my sensibility on the subject becomes dulled. "Resolutions ... are properly acts. And endeavouring to force upon our own minds a practical sense of virtue, or to beget in others that practical sense of it which a man really has himself, is a virtuous act. All these, therefore, may and will contribute towards forming good habits. But going over the theory of virtue in one's thoughts, talking well or drawing fine pictures of it, this is so far from necessarily or certainly conducing to form a habit of it in him who thus employs himself, that it may harden the mind in a contrary course, and render it gradually more insensible, *i.e.* form a habit of insensibility, to all moral considerations. For, from our very faculty of habits, passive impressions by being repeated grow weaker. Thoughts, by often passing through the mind, are felt less sensibly; being accustomed to danger begets intrepidity, *i.e.* lessens fear; to distress, lessens the passion of pity; to instances of others' mortality, lessens the sensible apprehension of our own. And from these two observations together, that practical habits are formed and strengthened by repeated acts, and that passive impressions grow weaker by being repeated upon us, it must follow that active habits may be gradually forming and strengthening by a course of acting upon such and such motives and excitements, whilst these motives and excitements themselves are, by proportionate degrees, growing less sensible, *i.e.* are continually less and less sensibly felt, even as the active habits strengthen." (*An.* 1.5.4.) Butler had little to learn from the author of *Oblomov*.

When we think of Butler, there is a natural disposition to call up at the same time the name of Berkeley. The periods of their lives were almost the same, both were bishops of the established church, both were outstanding philosophers and active Christian advocates. Indeed, the poetic fitness of connecting them struck Bartlett so forcibly that he devoted a substantial chapter in the *Life* to the career and writings of Butler's friend, Berkeley; though there is no evidence that they were more than casually acquainted. Butler, indeed, sampled tar water during his last illness, but we do not find that it was administered by the Bishop of Cloyne.

A systematic comparison of their philosophies could hardly be fruitful, for the fields of their special greatness do not coincide. But the subject of the *Analogy* has something in common with that of Berkeley's *Alciphron*, and it is instructive to remark the difference between the manner in which one writer and the other handles sceptics and infidels. The *Alciphron* is a lively, sparkling, and in some places charming work. It is directed against fashionable forms of infidelity, which Berkeley pursues, not only with ingenious reasoning, but with unsparing mockery and satire. No more quarter is given than in a debating society, and the laughs are all on Berkeley's side. This manner of writing is, no doubt, adapted to delight and fortify the orthodox, but can surely have little tendency to persuade the profane. In spite of the gravity and soberness which are the prevailing notes of all his writings, even Butler sometimes allows himself – in the *Sermons* more than in the *Analogy* – a little gentle rallying of "men of pleasure" and "those who are said to know the world". But the tone is unoffending and concessive, and is never calculated to furnish cheap triumphs to the writer's own party. Butler would rather persuade his opponents than score off them, he would rather persuade a little than not at all, and his style is that of a man who hopes, perhaps not very confidently, that those who do not take his side may attend, even if not earnestly or for long, to some part of his reasonings and admonitions.

CHAPTER 2

BUTLER'S THEORY OF HUMAN NATURE

§·1 · *The meaning of the word "nature"*

THE phrase "human nature" and its equivalents, which carry considerable weight in Butler's writings, may well be thought vague. It was not Butler's intention that they should remain vague. His careful analysis of the meaning of the word "nature" is to be found in the *Preface* and in *S.* 2: his general theory of human nature is set out most fully in the *Preface* and the first three sermons, and many further hints are to be found in other sermons, in the *Dissertation on virtue*, and in the *Analogy*.

The topic which Butler discusses under the name of "human nature" would nowadays be regarded as the business of psychologists. Butler had the good fortune to write in an age when the study of the mind had not yet been surrounded with the technical trappings of an exact science, and it was still permissible for a reflective man to talk good sense about human thoughts and feelings in generally intelligible language. But it was not part of his purpose to survey all the powers of the mind. Writing as a moral philosopher, he wished to recommend right conduct by showing that virtue corresponds to our nature and vice violates it (*Pr.* 12–13, etc.). He is therefore interested in those elements of a human person – impulses and appetites, capacities for happiness and misery, reflective powers – and those relations between the elements, which may lead to virtuous or vicious conduct, or which may enable him to distinguish one from the other.

The notion that good conduct is in harmony with man's nature, and ill conduct violates it – or even, to put it more strongly, that the goodness and badness of conduct is

[41]

constituted entirely by this correspondence of conduct with our nature, or the lack of it – is, as Butler remarks, no novelty. It is at least as old as the Stoics. But how are we to give such a meaning to the word "nature" as will make this claim intelligible? In the first place, any feature of the world may be called part of nature, and so any feature whatever of a person may be called part of that person's nature (*S.* 2.4–5). But when the word is used in this sense, it is absurd to speak of any kind of conduct as contrary to a man's nature: for his conduct will always be part of his nature. Since people are subject to inner conflicts, an act might conflict with part of a man's nature; but it would always be in conformity with part. Since no part is privileged, it would be absurd to speak of vice or wrongdoing as "breaking in upon" human nature.

But since a man's nature, in this first sense of the word, contains many impulses and motives – "principles" as Butler would say – which may conflict with one another, it is possible for one principle, temporarily or permanently, to dominate the rest. We might then (*S.* 2.6) describe a man's nature as consisting of the dominant part, and we should now be using the word "nature" in a second sense. But it would still be absurd, in this second sense, to speak of virtue and vice as consisting of conformity or lack of conformity with a man's nature. For in a virtuous man virtuous principles are dominant, and in a vicious man vicious principles: and every man, whatever he does, is necessarily and always following his nature.

These two senses of the word "nature" are mentioned by Butler only to be dismissed. It is essential to his design to make their dismissal clear from the start: when he speaks of following our nature he never means acting upon the impulse or "principle" which happens to be strongest at the moment, "as its turn happens to come" (*Pr.* 24).

There is, Butler maintains, a third sense of the word "nature", which both ancient and modern writers – he quotes the Stoics and St Paul – have probably had in mind, in speaking of nature as something with which our actions, as they are virtuous or vicious, may correspond or fail to correspond

§ 1 · MEANING OF "NATURE"

(*Pr.* 16). To explain this third sense we must look at Butler's own account of human nature.

A man's nature, so far as it determines his conduct, consists of elements or "principles" of several different types (*Pr.* 14–16): there are "appetites, passions, affections" in great variety; these may conflict with one another, and one may for a time be stronger than the others, and prevent their indulgence: there is also a power of surveying and appraising the various passions, and forming judgements for or against the indulgence of them. But man's nature is not adequately described by giving a list of these principles. It is a "constitution" or "economy", in which each part stands in determinate relations to the other parts: just as a watch consists, not merely of a collection of wheels, screws, and springs, but of these things so related in space that, in accordance with the laws of mechanics, the whole machine will serve to measure time. And just as a watch may be out of order, so may a human person.

So far as a man's conduct results from the interaction of various "principles", differing from one another in strength from time to time, his constitution is like that of "brute creatures" (*Pr.* 23). But there is an important difference. Man's internal principles form a hierarchy or system, in which they are related to one another not merely by differences in strength, and in the frequency with which one principle or another is in command. We have not given a complete description of his constitution until we have noted that one principle may be superior to another in a manner quite distinct from difference of strength, which Butler expresses by saying that it has "authority" (*S.* 2 and 3, esp. 3.9); or that it is superior in "kind" or "nature" (*Pr.* 15). And this authority or superiority is a quality which we can discover by scrutinising our "internal frame", just as we discover the existence of the passions, their harmony or discord, and their degrees of strength. When Butler wrote, the word 'introspection' had not yet come into use; although philosophical psychologists of course used introspective methods, the view that here was

[43]

a psychological technique which was distinct and *sui generis* had not yet arisen. But it is probably not too much of an anachronism to say that, in Butler's view, the internal economy, which includes the authority of one principle over another, is common to all normal men, and any of us can find it out by cool and careful introspection (*S.* 1.8; 2.1; 7.14: *D. on V.* 1).

We can now begin to discern the third sense of the word "nature" to which Butler wishes to draw attention. When a man acts on an "inferior", or less authoritative principle, and disregards a principle which is of more authority, he goes against his inner constitution as a whole, and may be said to be acting against his nature. When his action is in conformity with whatever principle has most authority, he acts according to his nature, even though some inferior principle may be disregarded (*S.* 2.14).

It is clear that here the word "nature" is not used in either of the senses noticed before. In the first sense, in which a man's nature is just the collection of all the elements which make him up, he acts partly according to his nature and partly against it, in both the cases supposed. In the second sense, he acts in both cases according to his nature, since to do so is, in that sense, to act on the principle which happens to be strongest. But Butler is introducing a third sense, in which a man's nature is followed in one case and violated in the other. If the principle which has most authority is not also the strongest, a man's nature as a whole is violated. His act is then "disproportionate to his nature" (*S.* 2.10).

§ 2 · *The hierarchy of human nature*

THE notion of authority, or of natural superiority of one principle to another, has to be introduced before we can see what Butler means when he speaks of human nature. We shall find that the notion is far from clear. Its difficulties will begin to appear when we review in more detail the various principles

§ 2 · HIERARCHY OF HUMAN NATURE

which, in Butler's view, make up the hierarchy of human nature.

The principles which have least authority are called by Butler "particular affections, passions, and appetites", or "particular movements towards ... particular external objects" (*Pr.* 35; *S.* 11.5). A passion or appetite is "a direct simple tendency towards such and such objects, without distinction of the means by which they are to be obtained" (*S.* 2.13). Examples taken at random are hunger; fear; resentment; compassion; sexual desire; love of society; desire for other people's esteem; and so on.

Butler does not explain how he distinguishes a "passion", an "appetite", and an "affection" from one another. Sometimes he uses all these words together, or two of them, to stand for a certain general class of human motives. They do not seem to be quite interchangeable. Hunger, for example, is an appetite, and it would seem incongruous, to Butler as much as to us, to call it a passion; desire of esteem is a passion, and it would seem strange to call it an appetite; and so on (*S.* 1.7 and fns.). In speaking of individual motives, Butler observes the congruities of ordinary speech. But it is not part of his purpose to analyse the psychological distinctions which underlie these varied names. In his view, all the passions, affections, and appetites occupy the same rank in man's constitution.

In what follows, the word "passion" will generally be used to stand for the whole class of passions, appetites, and affections.

Besides the particular passions, there are three principles which stand in places of special importance in the hierarchy: benevolence, self-love, and conscience or reflection. The position of benevolence is a little uncertain. Butler sometimes speaks as though it occupied a distinct rank, sometimes as though it were merely one of the particular passions. On the whole, his language leans more towards representing benevolence as one of the passions, but a passion which calls for special attention for a number of reasons.

[45]

CH. 2 · THEORY OF HUMAN NATURE

In the first place, Butler always sees a specially close connection between benevolence and general goodness of character. Although in particular cases, good will to others may be disproportionate and misdirected, and although we cannot safely regulate our conduct entirely by our judgement of what will bring most happiness, Butler is strongly inclined to think that the whole of goodness must, in some way, be ultimately reducible to benevolence. (Butler's views on the relation between benevolence and virtue will be considered more fully in chapter 5, § 2.)

Secondly, Butler wished to refute certain theories current, in his day perhaps even more than in ours, among "people who are said to know the world". One such theory is that there can never be a genuine desire to promote other people's well being, and that apparent good will towards others is illusory. Another is that, whether or not benevolent and public-spirited motives actually exist, *if* they exist they must conflict with one's own interests.

Against such theories, Butler insisted on the existence of benevolence, and its compatibility with self-love. (More will be said about these theories in chapter 4.)

Thirdly, Butler held that, although genuine benevolence does exist, it tends to be too weak in men. It stands alone among the passions in needing to be specially cultivated, and as a practical moralist Butler wished to give reasons for its cultivation (*Pr.* 40).

There is much less doubt about the position of self-love in the hierarchy than about that of benevolence. It is quite distinct from all the passions, and is of superior authority to all of them, with the possible exception of benevolence. Butler's references to self-love do not all seem, at first glance, altogether consistent with one another. Sometimes he gives the impression that it is of almost the highest authority, and scarcely distinguishable from conscience; sometimes that, though inferior to conscience, it is none the less a principle tending on the whole to virtue; and sometimes that it is as much a vicious as a virtuous principle. Most or all of the

§ 2 · HIERARCHY OF HUMAN NATURE

apparent inconsistency will disappear when the various references to self-love are considered in their contexts.

Contending against those who maintained that altrustic conduct was either impossible, or undesirable, Butler was perhaps not unwilling to startle his readers by making it appear that he also was, in his own way, an advocate of selfishness. There does not "appear any reason", he writes (*Pr.* 40), "to wish self-love were weaker in the generality of the world than it is. The influence which it has seems plainly owing to its being constant and habitual, which it cannot but be, and not to the degree or strength of it. Every caprice of the imagination, every curiosity of the understanding, every affection of the heart, is perpetually showing its weakness by prevailing over it. Men daily, hourly sacrifice the greatest known interest to fancy, inquisitiveness, love, or hatred, any vagrant inclination. The thing to be lamented is, not that men have so great regard to their own good or interest in the present world, for they have not enough; but that they have so little to the good of others." "In the common course of life, there is seldom any inconsistency between our duty and what is called interest: it is much seldomer that there is any inconsistency between duty and what is really our present interest; meaning by interest happiness and satisfaction. Self-love, then, ... does in general perfectly coincide with virtue, and leads us to one and the same course of life" (*S.* 3.8). The teaching exemplified in these passages is perhaps the most fundamental part of Butler's account of human nature.

About the position of conscience in the hierarchy there is no doubt. No "human creature can be said to act conformably to his constitution of nature unless he allows to that superior principle the absolute authority which is due to it" (*Pr.* 24). The doctrine of the "natural supremacy of conscience" is set out in *Sermons* 2 and 3. "You cannot form a notion of this faculty, conscience, without taking in judgement, direction, superintendency. This is a constituent part of the idea, that is, of the faculty itself: and to preside and govern, from the very economy and constitution of man, belongs to it. Had it strength

CH. 2 · THEORY OF HUMAN NATURE

as it has right, had it power as it has manifest authority, it would absolutely govern the world" (*S.* 2.14).

Butler often implies that conscience and self-love never conflict (*Pr.* 41; and *S.* 3.8, quoted above). But should they do so, there is no doubt that conscience is the "superior" principle (*Pr.* 26 and elsewhere).

This, then, is the bare structure of human nature. It is a hierarchy with three different levels: at the lowest level the passions, at the highest conscience, and in between self-love, possibly conjoined with benevolence. We shall now look more closely at the individual elements which occupy these ranks.

§ 3 · *The passions and their objects*

BUTLER often speaks of the passions as "movements towards *external* objects", in distinction from self-love, whose objects are "internal" (*Pr.* 35; *S.* 13.5). Self-love is a general desire for one's own happiness: it pursues "somewhat internal, our own happiness, enjoyment, satisfaction". If it seeks anything external, it never does so "for the sake of the thing, but only as a means of happiness or good: particular affections rest in the external things themselves" (*S.* 11.5).

The notion of self-love includes the avoidance of pain: but the positive activity inspired by self-love depends entirely on the existence of the passions; for "the very idea of interest or happiness consists in this, that an appetite or affection enjoys its object" (*Pr.* 37). Thus, in a given instance, it may be impossible for an observer to know how far an action is inspired by self-love, and how far by a particular passion (*Pr.* 36). But the distinction still exists, even if we cannot apply it. A man is acting from self-love in so far as he has considered to what extent his action will contribute to the satisfying of his passions in the long run, or as many of them as possible, and has come to the conclusion that it will promote those satisfactions on the whole.

Butler gives no analysis of the meaning of "external" and

§ 3 · THE PASSIONS

"internal", or of "object", or of the relation between a passion and an object. His language suggests that an object of someone's passion is internal if, and only if, it consists of or includes a state of feeling on the part of that person; and that otherwise it is external. Yet there must surely be passions whose objects are, in this sense, internal; for example, the desire to get rid of a persistent worry, or the appetite for thrills of various kinds. These are, in Butler's language, particular, and distinct from self-love. A man may go on the giant switchback at a fun fair for the sake purely of ecstatic sensations, with no thought at all of the act's probable influence on his happiness in the long run – from "passion" therefore.

Butler does not take much notice of the variety of relations in which the object of a passion might stand to the subject of it. He writes almost as though there were a single relation of possession. When a man is hungry (as Broad points out, *Five types*, p. 67), his appetite leads him, not merely to promote the existence of food, or its proximity to him, or its being brought within his control. He must eat it, and no other relation to food but eating would satisfy this particular appetite. But he does not eat the objects of ambition, or sympathy, or fear. He stands in a different relation to each of them. It appears that statements of such forms as "he desires X" are always elliptical: a fuller statement would be that he desires X to come into existence, or to multiply, or to come into some distinctive relation to himself.

Butler seems here to be accepting uncritically the colloquial use of the word "object", when it is combined with words standing for desires or purposive actions. It will not always be possible to follow his usage, and when something less elliptical is needed the word 'objective' will be used. An objective is the state of affairs which the passion, if unimpeded, tends to bring about. (A fuller analysis of the notion will be given below.) Thus, we shall say that the objective of hunger is the eating of food by the hungry man; the objective of love is loving association with the loved one; of compassion, the relieving of someone's distress; and so on.

CH. 2 · THEORY OF HUMAN NATURE

If we took Butler to imply that the objective of a passion is always external, it would hardly be possible to agree. We may have states of feeling of our own as objectives. But very often in order to produce the desired state of feeling it is necessary to bring about changes of other kinds: to get the thrills of speed I must board the switchback or the aeroplane; to relieve my anxieties I may judge it desirable to seek the advice of a psychiatrist; and so on. If we are prepared to speak very loosely of any people or things or happenings which I bring under my influence, in seeking to satisfy a passion, as the "objects" of it, we may nearly always be able to find an object which is external. But it is doubtful, even then, whether the external object can always be found. There may surely be passions whose objectives are sought through purely mental exertions, as in day-dreaming. We may concede to Butler that the objectives of self-love are internal in the sense explained, but we cannot deny that the objectives of particular passions may be internal also. The distinction between the passions and self-love will have to be found in the fact that the former are "particular", and self-love is "general" (*Pr. 36*). A man acts from self-love in so far as he is guided by "a general notion of interest", that is, of what will satisfy him most on the whole.

Butler argues, somewhat briefly, that the passions are "towards external things themselves, distinct from the pleasure arising from them", on the ground that "there could not be this pleasure, were it not for that prior suitableness between the object and the passions: there could be no enjoyment or delight from one thing more than another, from eating food more than from swallowing a stone, if there were not an affection or appetite to one thing more than another" (*S. 11.6*).

Now if by "the pleasure" Butler means the entire pleasurable experience which may constitute the satisfying of a desire, he seems here to be giving an argument against the contention that sometimes the object of a passion is internal. In this compressed and somewhat obscure passage, he seems to maintain, not merely, as against psychological hedonists,

[50]

§ 3 · THE PASSIONS

that some passions do not have pleasure as their object, but, far more sweepingly, that pleasure is never the object of a passion. And his reason is that the pleasure of satisfied desire could never arise unless there were a "prior suitableness" between the passion and an object. This suitableness consists of the fact that the object is desired, and the difference between two passions is a difference in their objects.

To judge the value of Butler's argument we must attempt an analysis of the relation between a passion and some other state of affairs which is expressed by saying that the latter is the 'objective' of the former; for Butler gives no analysis.

We can arrange human actions in a continuous series, having at its lower end reflex actions, and at its higher end those which are most deliberate and reflective. Near the lower end are impulsive actions, such as sudden outbursts of anger or joy. The most characteristic example of action prompted by "passions, affections or appetites" would come a little higher in the scale. A hungry man preparing or seeking food, even though he has not reflected on what he is doing in its relation to his needs and aims on the whole, can give some account of what he is doing. The causation of his conduct is to some extent conceptual; that is, he is prompted partly at least, by foresight or imagination of some state of affairs, for example eating a grilled chop, which his actions tend to bring about. We shall naturally describe this state of things by saying that a series of acts on his part, for example buying a chop from the butcher, lighting a gas burner, and so on, 'have as their object' the eating of the grilled chop, or that they are carried out 'for the sake of' the eating of the chop, or 'with a view to' it.

When this sort of formula is used to describe the relation between an earlier and a later series of actions – the chop-seeking and cooking series, in its relation to the chop-eating series – we may say that a 'teleological description' of the relation has been given, or that the earlier and the later series have been said to stand in a 'teleological relation'.

It will be a step towards analysing the notion of the objective of a passion if we can see in what circumstances the use of a teleological description is justified.

In the first place, it is clear that between the earlier and later series of actions – which we may call the 'means' series and the 'end' series – there is a causal relation. The means series tends to produce the end series unless it is interrupted, and unless it is ill devised in some way.

Secondly, in the case we have supposed, the person acting has some knowledge of this causal relation. If we ask him why he initiates the means series, he will probably be able to explain how his act is causally related to the rest of the means series, and how that in turn is causally related to the end series.

Thirdly, any change in the background situation which is likely to prevent the production of the end series tends to break off or to vary the means series. For example, if the gas supply is cut off, the hungry man will be likely to buy some kind of food which he can eat uncooked, instead of a chop.

In the example just given, both the means series and the end series consist of actions on the part of the agent. The end series, however, might consist of any state of affairs capable of being brought about or influenced by human conduct. Let us assume, with Butler and uncorrupted common sense, the existence of genuine altruistic impulses. Then, if a compassionate man seeks food to relieve someone else's hunger, the end series consists of the eating of food by someone other than the agent.

If the three foregoing conditions are fulfilled, a teleological description of the relation between the means series and the end series seems to be justified. But though these conditions are sufficient, they are not all necessary. And some alternative set of conditions might be sufficient.

That they are not all necessary may be seen if we reflect on the existence of ill conceived means and unconscious aims. If we see a man tying up a parcel with what is called a rogue's knot, we may, on other grounds, be entitled to say that his aim is to make the parcel hold together: but he has failed to find a suitable means. The first of the conditions set out above is

§ 3 · THE PASSIONS

not fulfilled. Nor can the second be fulfilled, for since the means series does not tend to produce the end series he cannot know that it does. A counterpart of the second condition is fulfilled: he believes that the means series will produce the end series, or at least hopes it may. And a counterpart of the third condition is fulfilled. Any stage in the course of events which makes it obvious that the end series will not be realised, for example the slipping apart of the ends of the string under strain, will tend to break off or vary the means series. The man will try other knots, or give up parcel-tying in despair.

Let us suppose, now, that someone has an engagement which requires him to catch a train at a certain time. It will take him an hour to reach the station, and one hour before the time of the train he starts to change his clothes, so making it probable that the train will be missed. And let us also suppose that, when he is offered an unexpected lift to the station in a car, he starts to repack his luggage. Here the first and third conditions are fulfilled. His sequence of actions tends to bring about the missing of the train; and when there is a change in the circumstances which might lead to his catching the train after all, he varies his course of action in a way which ensures that the train will still be missed. But the second condition is not properly fulfilled. He does not know, or at least he does not fully know and admit, that the means series tends to produce the end series. Or, as we sometimes say, he only knows it unconsciously or subconsciously.

There is a difference between the ill-conceived means and the unconscious aim. The teleological description seems fully appropriate to the former, but not quite appropriate to the latter. We have no hesitation in saying that the inept parcel-tier makes his unsuitable knots 'with the object of' making the parcel hold together. But it is a little misleading to say of the self-deceived train-misser that he delays his departure 'with a view to' missing the train: it seems desirable to add a qualification, and say that 'unconsciously' his object is to miss the train. This carries our analysis a little further. The agent's knowledge of, or belief in, the causal connection between the means

CH. 2 · THEORY OF HUMAN NATURE

series and the end series seems to be an essential part of the meaning of the teleological description. In order to justify the extension of the notion of purpose to cases in which this knowledge or belief is apparently absent, we have to make out that it is really present in some hidden part of the self.

Our results may be generalised as follows. Two sequences of happenings form a means series and an end series – or in other words a teleological relation holds between them – if, and only if, the first sequence consists of actions on the part of some agent; the agent believes – with or without good grounds – that the first sequence tends to produce the second sequence; and anything which weakens this belief tends also to break off or modify the first sequence.

It follows that when we give a teleological description of someone's conduct our description not only refers to his actual sequence of actions, and its consequences, but also involves a hypothesis as to the way in which his conduct would be modified if circumstances were to change. The fact that the hungry man procures and cooks a chop and then eats it justifies us provisionally in saying that the chop-seeking and cooking were done for the sake of the eating. But for a fuller justification we need that amount of general knowledge of the man which would entitle us to say how he would have acted in supposed circumstances, which did not in fact arise. Or, in other words, the teleological description implies, not only that a certain causal sequence occurred, but that it was produced by certain dispositions in the agent.

What light is thrown now on the relation which holds, not between a sequence of actions and an end series of events, but between a "passion" and its objective?

In the first place, it is clear that the indulging of a passion may vary from the impulsive snatching up of a desired morsel of food by a child to an ambitious man's lifelong contriving and scheming. And from these two examples it is clear that we must distinguish at least two senses in which such words as "passion" may be used. A passion may be a single relatively fleeting affective and conative state; or it may be a persistent

[54]

§ 3 · THE PASSIONS

tendency to experience affective and conative states of a certain type. Such words as 'hunger' usually stand for a passion in the former sense – by 'a hungry man' we do not usually mean a man frequently subject to food-seeking impulses, but a man who at a given moment is experiencing a food-seeking impulse. Such words as 'ambition', on the other hand, usually stand for a passion in the latter sense. A man's desire at 25 to get into Parliament, at 35 to become a minister, and at 45 to lead his party to power, are all, according to our common way of speaking, successive manifestations of his ambition.

Each of these successive phases in the development of ambition is made up of a series of relatively fleeting desires – to win the enthusiasm of an audience at an election meeting; to be praised for piloting a bill through a committee; and so on. These more fleeting desires are not properly called 'ambitions', though we may recognise them as ambitious desires if we see that they form part of a characteristic pattern in a man's life. A man's ambition consists in the fact that these desires for ends of the same general type play a larger part in his whole life history than in most people's.

It will not usually be necessary to keep strictly in mind the difference between these two senses of such words as 'passion': but for the moment it will be convenient to speak of 'occurrent passions', such as the impulse to snatch up a piece of food, and 'continuant passions', such as ambition.

For our present purpose we need not decide the final analysis of the basic concepts of psychology: we need not decide, for example, whether, as behaviourists hold, all references to states of consciousness ought to be analysed in terms of observable physical happenings. Thus we need not decide whether the conceptual element in the relation between a passion and its objective ought to disappear in analysis. An occurrent passion may or may not manifest itself in conduct in an obvious way. Some lovers never tell their love, and some hungry people deliberately go without food, or do not seek it because they know that, at the time, there is none to be had. This does not imply that no physical symptoms of the passion exist at all, for no doubt they do; but it follows that we cannot define the relation between the passion and its objective as consisting simply of its tendency to produce a means series of actions teleologically related to the objective. A series of food-seeking or wooing actions is one way in which love or hunger may be manifested, but only one of many. And we cannot provide, from the resources of common knowledge, a catalogue of all the possible outward manifestations of a passion: that could only be done as a result of much empirical research.

It seems, then, that we must use unanalysed psychological concepts, in our account of the relation between a passion and its objective. In the first place, it seems clear that every passion above the reflex level involves, in some degree, the thought of an objective. It would be paradoxical to say of a man that he is hungry but has no thought of food; that he is in love but never thinks of the woman he loves; or that he is eager to win an election, yet gives no thought to the voters. If we were speaking of a continuant passion, it would not be absurd to say that he does not always think of the objective: that is usually the case. But in so far as we are referring to an occurrent passion, we must be implying that the ambitious man, at the time when he is subject to the passion, is thinking of fame or power, the lover of the beloved.

Secondly, the thought has a certain tone, attractive or repellent. (Fears and aversions must be included among Butler's "passions, affections and appetites".) If the lover's thought of his loved one were coldly neutral, we should say he was out of love for the moment: if a man can think of food with indifference, his hunger has ceased.

Thirdly, there must be some disposition, however slight, to begin a series of actions related teleologically, or believed to be related teleologically, to the objective. The hungry man seeks food if opportunity offers, and if his food-seeking disposition is not inhibited by some other, an ascetic resolution for example.

That the third condition is necessary will appear if we compare a passion, in Butler's sense, with some exercise of the

§ 3 · THE PASSIONS

imagination. Consider, for example, the state of mind of a man contemplating a Utopia. The first condition is fulfilled, and so, very probably, is the second. But it would not be appropriate to say that he desires or fears the state of things he is imagining if he has no disposition to promote it or avert it, or if he does not believe that any action of his can affect the matter. Or if we are to say that he desires it, if, for instance, we are to apply the word 'desire' to the state of a child who says 'I wish I had a million pounds', or 'a magic carpet', we shall have to distinguish between idle desires or longings, and effective desires. Only effective desires are included among Butler's "passions, affections, and appetites".

If this account of an objective is on the right lines, the analysis of the relation between a means series and an end series has been absorbed into the analysis of the relation between an occurrent passion and an objective. When we say that the objective of hunger is the eating of food, we imply, not that the person experiencing the hunger actually initiates a series of food-seeking actions, but that he tends to do so in the absence of any counteracting cause.

The analysis of the notion of a continuant passion seems easy. An ambitious man is a man subject to frequent and intense occurrent passions whose objectives are fame or power in various forms. A benevolent man is subject to frequent and strong occurrent passions whose objectives consist of some other person's happiness. In general, a continuant passion consists of a disposition to experience occurrent passions of some one type to a conspicuous degree. A continuant passion is much the same as what is often called a 'trait of character'.

By distinguishing between occurrent and continuant passions, we can dispose of an objection to Butler's treatment of benevolence which Professor Broad raises. Butler cites the existence of compassion, and of paternal and filial affection, as proofs of the existence of benevolence. Broad objects (*Five types*, p. 72) that "paternal affection is just as much a particular impulse as hunger", and "can no more be identified with benevolence than hunger can be identified with self-

[57]

CH. 2 · THEORY OF HUMAN NATURE

love". Each of these examples may be taken as either continuant or occurrent: a man may feel an isolated impulse to relieve someone's distress, or he may be conspicuously subject to such impulses. Similarly he may feel an impulse of affection, on some one occasion, towards his parents or his children; or he may feel such impulses habitually. We should not call a man benevolent on the ground of an isolated impulse, for the word stands for a continuant disposition. Nor should we call him benevolent if he were habitually kindly towards some limited class of people, but not at all towards the mass of mankind. But benevolence is a matter of degree, and is recognized as such by Butler. "The thing to be lamented", as he says in the famous passage already quoted, "is not that men have so great regard to their own good or interest in the present world, for they have not enough; but that they have so little to the good of others." A man is to be called benevolent if he has a "habitual temper of benevolence", as Butler puts it (*S*. 9.12), that is, if he habitually feels and acts on benevolent impulses, and if there is no great restriction on the persons towards whom they are directed. But if he sometimes, however rarely, feels benevolent impulses towards some people, however few, although he is not to be called a benevolent man, the principle of benevolence exists in him in some degree. Broad, in insisting that benevolence is a "general" principle, seems to imply that there is some continuant passion having for its objective or objectives other people's well-being, and not manifesting itself in occurrent passions whose objectives are particular changes in the condition of individual persons. It may be so. But there is little or no evidence that this was Butler's meaning. He often uses such phrases as "benevolence towards particular persons" (*Pr*. 39). In *Sermon* 11 he seems to class benevolence consistently among "particular passions": he seems to draw little distinction between benevolence and "love of our neighbour", that is (*S*. 12.3) of "that part of mankind ... which comes under our immediate notice, acquaintance, and influence, and with which we have to do". In *Sermon* 1.6, fn. he seems to

§ 3 · THE PASSIONS

identify benevolence with "good-will in one man towards another". He does not appear ever to describe benevolence as a "general principle". In *Sermon* 12 he speaks of "the general temper of mind which the *due* love of our neighbour would form us to" (*S.* 12.20). This general temper is directed by "reason" or "reflection", which "lead us to consider distant consequences, as well as the immediate tendency of an action" (*S.* 12.27): and he is prepared to suppose that benevolence so directed may include the whole of virtue (*S.* 12.25–32), though in other places, as we shall see in chapter 5, he qualifies this suggestion a good deal. Similarly, in *S.P.* 6.3, he speaks of "a settled endeavour to promote, according to the best of our judgement", the "real lasting good" of our fellow creatures. There is nothing here which need imply that the virtuous benevolence of which Butler speaks consists of anything more than habitual cultivation of benevolent impulses towards particular people, under the guidance of conscience.

§ 4 · *The distinction between self-love and the particular passions*

WE have seen reason to reject Butler's claim that the objects of a particular passion are always external, and we cannot therefore distinguish these passions from self-love in terms of externality and internality. But we can retain the distinction which Butler expresses by his use of the word "particular", and of such phrases as "a general notion of interest" to indicate the objective of self-love (*Pr.* 36).

Butler's most typical statements about self-love concern what he also calls "cool self-love", "cool and reasonable concern" for oneself, "reasonable self-love", "cool consideration that" an action "will be to my own advantage", "general desire of happiness", "manifest and real interest", and so on. It "belongs to man as a reasonable creature, reflecting upon his own interest or happiness" (*S.* 11.5). He sometimes contrasts self-love, in this most typical sense, with "supposed interest", or "supposed self-love", that is, with people's false notions of what will bring them happiness: sometimes also – and this is harder to reconcile, as we shall see, with his general account of self-love – with "immoderate self-love" (*S.* 11.9), or "unreasonable and too great regard to ourselves", "over-fondness for ourselves" (*S.* 10.6).

Self-love in the typical sense is exercised when a man reflects on his own nature, as containing various passions in various degrees of strength, and the situation in which he is placed, and reaches a considered judgement as to the course of action which will satisfy his passions as fully as possible. In the absence of the particular passions, self-love would have no positive content. The element of desire in self-love has as its objective a man's own happiness. "Happiness or satisfaction consists only in the enjoyment of those objects which are by nature suited to our several appetites, passions, and affections" (*S.* 11.9). "Take away these affections and you leave self-love absolutely nothing at all to employ itself about; no end or object for it to pursue, excepting only that of avoiding pain" (*Pr.* 37).

The exception mentioned in the last sentence is never developed by Butler. But it may be fitted into the general scheme. We may think of self-love as, on its conative side, partly desire and partly aversion – desire for happiness and aversion from unhappiness and pain. It comes into play only when a man reflects coolly enough not to be dominated by the impulses of the moment. These impulses may consist, not only of occurrent passions such as Butler usually chooses for his examples, but of occurrent aversions. A man may feel fear of physical injury, for example from a mad bull or an armed robber or a house on fire; dislike of a boring social gathering from which he wishes to escape; anxious dread of poverty and its accompaniments, or ill health, or professional failure; and so on. So far as he acts relatively unreflectingly under the influence of one of these aversions, or counter-passions, self-love does not come into play. But if he reflects coolly he may perceive that he will serve his own interests best by resisting

§ 4 · SELF-LOVE AND THE PASSIONS

one of these impulses: for example, that he is more likely to save his life if he waits for the fire brigade than if he jumps from the top floor of a burning building: or that he is more likely to make and keep friends if he tolerates a certain amount of boredom instead of making his escape whenever he feels the impulse to do so. Here the particular aversions or counter-passions come under the reflective scrutiny of self-love in just the same way as the positive passions.

Self-love may be defective in strength. As Butler remarks in a passage already quoted in § 2 of this chapter, "the influence which it has seems plainly owing to its being constant and habitual, which it cannot but be, and not to the degree or strength of it" (*Pr.* 40).

Butler's language suggests that self-love varies in one dimension only. But this seems too simple. There seem to be several different ways in which self-love might be relatively ineffective. The general desire for one's own happiness, even when it came into play, might as a rule be weaker than the prevailing passion of the moment; or the ability to reflect coolly and realistically on the tenor of one's life might be small; or the knowledge and judgement of men and affairs which would make reflection fruitful might be lacking. Either or both of the first two shortcomings would imply that self-love was a relatively feeble check on the passions. If the third possibility were realised, even if a man's general desire for his own happiness were vigorous, and his reflection persistent, his ill-advised self-love would still often miss its objective.

We may take it that in Butler's view a "due degree" of self-love requires both a considerable power of cool reflection and a sufficient conative drive to overcome a prevailing passion in case of need. He probably assumed that most, if not all, men could reflect well enough on their own interests, if they once set themselves to do so; and that with reflection the general desire for happiness would gain sufficient force. But the third requirement – that self-love should be enlightened by knowledge and good judgement – he seems to have entirely overlooked. He has indeed a good deal to say about self-deception. But that is a malady of reflection, which, in Butler's view, would be overcome by more strenuous and candid self-scrutiny. No amount of effort and candour will remove handicaps in respect of intelligence, education, and knowledge of the world. Butler's hope that an extension of cool self-love would bring men much nearer to virtue might have been weakened if he had recognised that an ill-advised self-lover might do no better for himself than a man "abandoned in what is called the way of pleasure" (*Pr.* 40).

§ 5 · *The relation between self-love and good conduct*

BUTLER often says that self-love, even if the conduct it prompts does not coincide exactly with the conduct which conscience would prompt, tends on the whole the same way as conscience. "Self-love, though confined to the interest of the present world, does in general perfectly coincide with virtue, and leads us to one and the same course of life" (*S.* 3.8). He recognizes that this may seem a paradox, and that it is commonly thought that there is some opposition between virtue and interest, self-love being more a vicious than a virtuous principle (*S.* 11.2). Butler does not give a connected explanation of the existence of this vulgar error. But we can collect from a number of passages what his explanation would be.

In the first place, there are various intellectual confusions. There is no doubt that service to others, though not the whole of virtue, forms a substantial part of a good life. "The common virtues and the common vices of mankind may be traced up to benevolence, or the want of it", though "there are certain dispositions of mind, and certain actions, which are in themselves approved or disapproved by mankind, abstracted from the consideration of their tendency to the happiness or misery of the world" (*S.* 12.31, and fn.). And men mistakenly assume that to pursue *A* and to pursue *B* must always be mutually exclusive alternatives, so that if a man pursues someone else's

§ 5 · SELF-LOVE AND GOOD CONDUCT

happiness it follows that he is not, by the same course of action, pursuing his own (*S*. 11.18). This assumption is supported by a mistaken analogy between enjoyment and property, and confusion of enjoyment with means to enjoyment (*S*. 11.11–19). It is true that property is one of the means to enjoyment, and that the more of it a man gives away the less he has: but it does not follow that he has less enjoyment. This assumption of the mutual exclusiveness of self-love and service to others could only be made by those who have failed to notice that benevolence, sympathy, and other "public" passions, are just as much part of a man's nature as the "private" passions (*S*. 1.6, 7). "Does not all this kind of talk go upon supposition that our happiness in this world consists in somewhat quite distinct from regards to others?" (*S*. 3.7). This false supposition leads men to ignore another fact of their own nature – that in general a benevolent temper of mind is agreeable and a malevolent temper of mind disagreeable. "Let it not be taken for granted that the temper of envy, rage, resentment yields greater delight than meekness, forgiveness, compassion and good will: especially when it is acknowledged that rage, envy, resentment are in themselves mere misery; and the satisfaction arising from the indulgence of them is little more than relief from that misery; whereas the temper of compassion and benevolence is itself delightful; and the indulgence of it by doing good affords new positive delight and enjoyment" (*S*. 3.8; and *S*. 11.14–15).

This complication of mistakes gives men the impression that benevolent and other virtuous conduct requires a complete neglect of one's own interests, a course of action to which no need in one's own nature corresponds: hence "that scorn which one sees rising upon the faces of people who are said to know the world, when mention is made of a disinterested, generous, or public-spirited action" (*Pr*. 38). "The sum total of our happiness" is "supposed to arise from riches, honours, and the gratification of sensual appetites" (*S*. 11.15). This is the common talk of the world (*S*. 11.2 and elsewhere), and it is supported by the philosophical theories of psychological egoists, such as Hobbes. And those who thoughtlessly accept this false analysis of their own nature which holds the field will be biased against their own best interests. They will, perhaps, the more easily fall victims to the various distorted forms of self-love, which Butler describes as "immoderate self-love" (*S*. 11.9); "unreasonable and too great regard to ourselves, overfondness for ourselves, false selfishness" (*S*. 10.6); "partial, false self-love" (*S*. 9.25). And even without the influence of false theories and current notions, men are prone to deceive themselves (*S*. 10, and elsewhere). Men are too easily satisfied that all is well with their character and conduct, from lack of reflection, or self-partiality (*S*. 10.2, 3).

It is hard to be sure that Butler is altogether consistent here. If, as he often tells us, self-love is on the whole too weak in mankind, and would, if it were stronger, make them both better and happier, it is hard to understand how self-love can also be immoderate. If a man sits down in a cool hour "to consider how he may become most easy to himself, and attain the greatest pleasure he can" (*S*. 11.15), he may certainly reach wrong conclusions from lack of coolness, and the interruption of "favourite passions"; or from lack of knowledge and good judgement; but it is hard to see how he could do so from excess of self-love, as self-love was previously defined. He might, indeed, be led astray by false theories, which led him to ignore the existence in himself, for example, of kindly and sympathetic impulses, and the agreeableness of satisfying them. But since clear-sighted reflection is part of the notion of self-love, his failure to discern the falsity of those theories would be an instance of defective, not excessive self-love.

It must be admitted, then, that Butler has at the best expressed himself loosely. It seems possible that when he spoke of "overfondness for ourselves", and so on, he had in mind a distinction which is not expressly drawn, between a man's attitude to his own character and course of life as it has been, and is at the moment of reflection, and his attitude to the shaping of his life in the future. On this interpretation, self-

§ 5 · SELF-LOVE AND GOOD CONDUCT

partiality would be retrospective, while self-love in the primary sense would be prospective. In the exercise of self-love in the primary sense, the cool consideration "how to become most easy to themselves", most men will find something to amend in their past and present habits. But a man's attitude to his past and present self often has the "friendship and real kindness" inspired by a trusted friend (*S.* 10.3), and he is blinded to what, in his own interests, needs amendment. "Immoderate self-love" or "overfondness for ourselves" would then consist of excessive attachment to our existing scheme of life; it would not be excess of self-love in the primary sense, but an obstacle to its working. There would be two species of false self-love, that which comes from retrospective self-partiality, and that which comes from acceptance of false generalisations as to the best method of "attaining the greatest pleasure one can"; and these two errors might well interact, so that the "profligate men" who are "so greatly mistaken, when they affirm they are wholly governed by interestedness and self-love" (*An.* 1.5.13, fn.), would be misled both by excessive complacency about their settled way of life and by a false estimate of its happy tendency.

But given that self-love, in the primary meaning of the phrase, cannot be immoderate, in the sense of reaching a pitch where it defeats its own ends, that it is quite distinct from retrospective self-partiality, and that it may require a man to recognise in himself "public" as well as "private" passions, and the pleasures he may gain by satisfying them, is not Butler rather too confident of the virtuous tendency of self-love? Although in Butler's view benevolence is not the whole of virtue, and may indeed even take vicious forms, on the whole its tendency is good, and we may take what Butler has to say of the relation between benevolence and self-love as a fair test of the plausibility of his account of the relation between self-love and good conduct in general. Butler shows successfully that there is no necessary conflict between self-love and benevolence, that their being distinct does not imply that they are opposed. "Benevolence is not more unfriendly to self-interest than any other particular passion whatever" (*Pr.* 35). But Butler goes further, claiming that "benevolence and self-love . . . are so perfectly coincident that the greatest satisfactions to ourselves depend upon our having benevolence in a due degree" (*S.* 1.6). We seem to have passed here from the statement that benevolence is compatible with the exercise of self-love to the statement that it is necessary to it.

In questioning this contention, we are forced to question at the same time one of Butler's fundamental assumptions, on which his method of analysis rests. He assumed great uniformity in human nature. "If it be said that there are persons in the world who are in great measure without the natural affections towards their fellow-creatures; there are likewise instances of persons without the common natural affections to themselves: but the nature of man is not to be judged of by either of these, but by what appears in the common world, in the bulk of mankind" (*S.* 1.13; and *S.* 2.1). This is as far as Butler ever goes in recognising the diversity of human dispositions. The point is seldom expressly referred to: but the tacit assumption that what is found in the bulk of mankind is, in essentials, the same can often be seen. The exceptions, which Butler admits in the passage quoted, impress him no more than we are commonly impressed by the tacit exclusion, in many of our generalisations, of idiots or lunatics.

The question whether the "public" passions are so uniformly vigorous in all or almost all mankind that cool self-love would always lead to their cultivation and exercise is, as Butler would recognise, "a mere question of fact or natural history" (*S.* 1.6, fn.). Such a question is settled, in Butler's view (*l.c.*), by one or all of three methods: observation or introspection; inferring the "principle" of an action from the action; and the testimony of mankind. By all these methods it can be proved – and we need not dispute it – "that there is some degree of benevolence amongst men" (*l.c.*). But all that has been proved is what logicians call an instantial proposition, not a universal generalisation. Butler does not seem to have noticed that, by proving the existence in himself, or in such

§ 5 · SELF-LOVE AND GOOD CONDUCT

other men as he has observed or learnt about from testimony – even if they are a large number – of effective "public" passions, he has only gone a little way towards proving their existence in all or nearly all mankind.

The point is important because Butler seeks to give a double support to virtue. He wishes to prove, even to those who are deaf to conscience, that if only they reflect steadily on the means of forwarding their own happiness, they will find that they lie, partly at least, "in the exercise of charity, in the love of their neighbour, in endeavouring to promote the happiness of all they have to do with, and in the pursuit of what is just" (*S.* 11.15). The proof consists of careful examination of "the inward frame of man" (*S.* 2.1). Although he does not say so expressly, Butler often gives the impression that his method is analogous to the method used by an anatomist in finding out the structure and functions of a living body. An anatomist, after examining a small number of specimens, will very probably conclude that the arrangement of organs which he has found is common to the whole species. But reliable inference from a few specimens to a whole species is only possible when certain taxonomic generalisations are already well established. Having discovered that a few females of a given mammalian species have four udders, he will conclude that the same is true of the whole species, because constancy in the number of udders is already well established for mammalian species in general, whereas because a few specimens of a species have brown hair he would not dream of concluding that all members of the species have. As logicians have often observed, it is already well established that the formation of the principal organs is highly correlated with general bodily structure, but not that colour of hair is correlated with general bodily structure. But man's moral anatomy is not yet so well established that, having discovered the nature of the various passions in some individuals, we can safely conclude that it is the same in all.

Thus, while Butler does make very plausible the contention that, in some, perhaps in many men, an increase of cool self-

CH. 2 · THEORY OF HUMAN NATURE

love would be conducive to virtue, he does not give very solid grounds for holding that it would in all or nearly all of mankind. On the other hand, Butler's guess is as good as another man's, and we cannot give solid grounds for saying that he is wrong in assuming the virtuous tendency of self-love to be nearly universal. And since self-love is known to be conducive to virtue in many men, we cannot be sure that, in an individual taken at random, it is not conducive to virtue. A writer who seeks, not only to satisfy intellectual curiosity, but, like Butler, to edify and do good, is therefore justified in assuming that his readers or hearers are capable of being made better by a cool appeal to their interests. If they are susceptible to such an appeal he will do good, and if they are not he will not do harm.

Butler's general assumption is not, of course, that the economy of the passions is exactly the same in all men. He fully recognises diversities of character and temperament. But he assumes that in all, or almost all men, the "public" passions are strong enough, and the satisfactions arising from them lively enough, to make a virtuous course of life conducive to the individual's own happiness.

We shall need to refer to this assumption again, and we may name it the principle of 'uniformity of interest'.

We have now set out the general structure of human nature, as Butler conceives it. In the following chapter the idea of conscience, and of its authority, will be examined. Butler's attitude to the various doctrines of selfishness, already noticed in the present chapter, will be considered more fully in chapter 4.

CHAPTER 3

CONSCIENCE AND ITS AUTHORITY

§ 1 · *Butler's assumptions: the distinction between uniformity of conscience and uniformity of duty*

"THERE is a superior principle of reflection or conscience in every man, which distinguishes between the internal principles of his heart, as well as his external actions; which passes judgement upon himself and them, pronounces determinately some actions to be in themselves just, right, good, others to be in themselves evil, wrong, unjust; which, without being consulted, without being advised with, magisterially exerts itself, and approves or condemns him, the doer of them, accordingly" (*S.* 2.8).

"We have a capacity of reflecting upon actions and characters ... and on doing this we naturally and unavoidably approve some actions, under the peculiar view of their being virtuous and of good desert, and disapprove others, as vicious and of ill desert" (*D. on V.* 1).

"Nor is it at all doubtful in the general what course of action this faculty ... approves ... It is that which all ages and all countries have made profession of in public; it is that which every man you meet puts on the show of; it is that which the primary and fundamental laws of all civil constitutions over the face of the earth ... enforce the practice of upon mankind; namely justice, veracity, and regard to common good" (*D. on V.* 1).

These passages illustrate, what may readily be illustrated from many others, three fundamental assumptions contained in Butler's theory of conscience. We may name them 'the authority of conscience', 'the uniformity of conscience', and 'the uniformity of duty'. Some account of the notion of authority, or "natural supremacy", has already been given in

[69]

chapter 2, § 2. The principle of the uniformity of conscience is akin to the principle of uniformity of interest, which will be noticed again in chapter 4, § 2. Just as all men, if they reflected coolly on their own nature, would find that justice, veracity and public spirit were the means to their own happiness; so all men, if they reflected, would find that the very same course of life – the just, honest and benevolent life – was prescribed for them authoritatively by something in themselves – all men, or nearly all, at all times and places.

The principle of uniformity of duty is never stated by Butler so explicitly as the other two. It is certain that he held it, but he does not stress it because it had not occurred to him that it might be questioned, as it has been by modern relativists. Its critics have sometimes, we may suspect, confused it with the uniformity of conscience. They have supposed, on what seem to be strong grounds, that modern psychological and anthropological discoveries have disproved the uniformity of conscience, and they have wrongly supposed that diversity of conscience entails diversity of duty. Let us imagine that in a certain community the robbing and cheating of strangers is universally approved of, and its omission condemned. Since in other communities hospitality to strangers is enjoined, there is ostensible diversity of conscience as regards the treatment of strangers. And this state of affairs is often loosely expressed by saying 'in one place it's a duty to rob a stranger, and in another place it's a duty to befriend him'. But what is meant here, of course, is not that in a certain place robbing strangers actually is a duty, but only that it's generally regarded as a duty. If we believe that it is right to befriend strangers, we are free to hold that those who preach and practise the robbing of strangers are wrong, that they are morally unenlightened, and have failed to discern their duty in this matter, which is the same as the duty of any other men anywhere else. We are free, that is, to maintain the uniformity of duty: we are also free to maintain its diversity; but its diversity cannot be proved from the existence of conflicting distributions of approval and disapproval.

§ 1 · BUTLER'S ASSUMPTIONS

The principles of uniformity of duty and of conscience do not require that the detailed rules which are, or ought to be, observed in daily life should be the same everywhere, without regard to circumstances. For example, the established attitude to the use of water in arid countries is different from what it is in well watered countries. In the former, emphasis is laid on the duty of not wasting water, in the latter on the duty of using enough for cleanliness and health. But there is no diversity of conscience, if the water-savers and the water-spenders are prepared to explain their rules about water as applications of a single general principle to dissimilar situations – for example, a utilitarian principle to the effect that natural resources should be used for the greatest happiness of the greatest number. And there would be no diversity of duty if that were a correct account of the matter – that is, if there were a single true moral generalisation from which the different rules for the two situations could be derived.

To distinguish between the principles of uniformity of conscience and uniformity of duty would be superfluous only if a certain questionable theory were true – the theory that the sole criterion of duty is compliance with the moral code of one's own place and time. In that case, the conditions under which either principle would be true or false would be the same. If there were conflict between the basic assumptions of various moral codes, that conflict would constitute diversity of conscience, and it would follow from it that duty was diverse: and contrariwise, if all moral codes were fundamentally in harmony, both conscience and duty would be uniform. But the opinion that it must always be wrong to infringe the moral code of one's place and time is far from plausible: to say the least, we cannot take it for granted, and we must therefore retain and insist on the distinction between uniformity of conscience and of duty.

Some modern writers hold that the notions of truth and falsity are not properly applicable to moral principles. To meet their views, we should have to reformulate our statement of the uniformity of duty. We can still express the matter quite

[71]

clearly, provided it is admitted that there is a distinction between making a moral judgement oneself and reporting someone else's moral judgements. In that case, when we speak about the duties of people in other societies than our own, when we praise or blame them, or describe their conduct as right or wrong, we are making moral judgements of our own. We may also be in a position to know what moral judgements would have been made by the people in question and the other members of their society. These moral judgements might differ radically from ours. In that case we shall have to recognise diversity of conscience, but we need not admit diversity of duty. For in our own judgements about the conduct of people at different places and times we may always apply the same standards. We may, for instance, condemn those who rob strangers and who approve of robbing strangers: and in that case we shall be holding to uniformity of duty while recognising diversity of conscience.

It is difficult for modern people to accept uniformity of conscience as confidently as Butler did, unless the generalisation is tacitly confined to a small part of mankind; to civilised men, for example, or to those who have inherited Christian traditions. Since Butler's time the notion of social evolution has come to be generally accepted; we think it a truism that the moral code of a society forms a single fabric with its institutions and economic life, and that it is as much subject to growth as any other part of the fabric. And it seems to be fairly well established that universalistic moral codes, in which, theoretically at least, all mankind are to be treated alike, are a comparatively recent growth. In earlier moralities, and probably in those which still prevail in many parts of the world, a man's primary obligations are connected with some limited group, and its members – a family, or a tribe, or a city, or a nation, or a social class – and in respect of those outside this group he has either no obligations, or obligations of a quite different kind.

If we reject the assumption of uniformity of conscience, we seem at first sight compelled to reject also at least one of the

§ 1 · BUTLER'S ASSUMPTIONS

other two assumptions, the authority of conscience and the uniformity of duty. For the authority of conscience, whatever its exact analysis may be, must surely imply that conscience is a reliable guide to duty. And this, if conscience is diverse and duty uniform, it cannot be. We can suppose that diverse consciences authoritatively prescribe diverse duties, or that since the uniform course of duty is often misconceived by men's consciences, conscience as such has no authority. But one of the two principles must give way.

§ 2 · *The meaning of "conscience"*

WHETHER this reasoning is decisive will only appear when we have considered just what is meant by "conscience" and its "authority". And here we are faced with a fundamental question which Butler treats in an oddly slighting and perfunctory way. Having asserted the existence of a "moral approving and disapproving faculty", in *D. on V.* 1, he goes on "whether called conscience, moral reason, moral sense, or Divine reason; whether considered as a sentiment of the understanding or as a perception of the heart; or, which seems the truth, as including both".

The characteristic language of the *Sermons* has already been illustrated above. Conscience is a power of reflecting on intentions and actions, by which we discern their moral qualities and the obligations under which we lie. But as to the nature of a moral quality, and the manner of discerning it, we only have dark hints from Butler.

We must try to make explicit what is implicit in these hints: although such an attempt as that which follows is bound to involve some historical falsification. The only method open to us is to deduce, from a writer's express statements, consequences which he could not consistently reject unless he rejected the premisses. But writers are not always consistent, and do not always distinctly consider all the deductions which might be drawn from their statements. If a writer' sattention were drawn to one of these deductions, he might reject it, and prefer to modify the premiss rather than accept the conclusion. Even if we feel safe in guessing that, had he contemplated a certain consequence, he would have accepted it, we ought not without qualification to set down as part of his views what we deduce from his expression of them. The most we can say, without distortion and anachronism, is that if Butler, or whoever it may be, had developed his doctrine further he might have done so on the lines we suggest.

The following points are clear from Butler's express statements.

1. By the exercise of conscience men find out what is right and wrong, or good and bad, in conduct and character.

2. This is different from finding out, in the exercise of self-love, "how a man may become perfectly easy with himself", even though the course of conduct proposed to him by self-love may very nearly coincide with that which is right and good.

3. The result reached by one man, through the exercise of conscience, is substantially the same as that which would be reached by any other man, with reference to a similar situation.

4. To the results reached by conscience belongs the special quality which Butler calls "authority". (This seems to imply that when, in the exercise of conscience, I recognise an action to be right, this recognition constitutes, of itself, a reason for doing the action: though Butler does not express the point in this way.)

5. Although men always have a reason for doing what conscience enjoins, that is, authority always belongs to conscience, they do not always do it.

From points (3) and (4) we may deduce the principle which has already been named 'uniformity of duty': a more general name would be 'uniformity of values'. In given circumstances, the courses of action to which the authority of conscience attaches are the same for all men. There must, then, be a range of true universal propositions, each of which is to the effect that every state of affairs which is in non-moral respects of a certain character would have a certain moral character. We

§ 2 · MEANING OF "CONSCIENCE"

may call such propositions 'moral universals'. The qualities which are named by such words as 'good', 'bad', 'right', 'wrong', and so on, may be called 'moral qualities'. A moral universal, then, asserts that whatever has a certain non-moral characteristic also has a certain moral quality. A characteristic related in this way to a moral quality may be called a 'value-bearing quality'.

Let us suppose that a certain act of breaking a promise is wrong. It follows that any exactly similar act of breaking a promise would be wrong. It does not follow that another act of breaking a promise would be wrong if there were some morally relevant difference between the two cases – a difference, for example, in the content of the promise, or the manner in which it came to be made, or the expected consequences of keeping or breaking it. Thus, the value-bearing qualities of a subject, on which its moral qualities depend, may have wide ramifications – theoretically they might include its very remote consequences, or even the relation in which the subject stood to anything else in the universe. But we need not suppose that, in order that two acts of promise-breaking shall be wrong, they must be exactly alike. There may be some quite limited group of qualities which they have in common, which are the value-bearing qualities, and it may be true that every act of promise-breaking with this limited group of qualities would be wrong. This last truth would be a moral universal. The characteristic of being an act of breaking a promise in such and such circumstances would be a value-bearing quality. The truth that a particular instance of the value-bearing quality, an individual act of promise-breaking, for example, is wrong, may be called a 'moral singular'.

Clearly conscience as conceived by Butler must include the power of responding to moral singulars. For in its "magisterial" activity it directs, or can direct, men's daily and hourly conduct. But Butler's deliberately elusive language does not authorise us to say that an act of conscience is primarily cognitive – a "perception" or act of "understanding" – rather than affective or conative – a "sentiment" or a movement of

[75]

CH. 3 · CONSCIENCE

the "heart". Although, when conscience operates, a moral singular must be involved, we are not entitled to say that the act of conscience is merely the noting or discovering of a moral singular. There seem to be two elements which, as a minimum, it must contain: (1) awareness of a value-bearing quality; (2) inclination towards or away from the subject of the value-bearing quality – love of what is good and hatred of or distaste for what is bad. If we think of these two elements as interpenetrating one another, so that it would be fitter to speak, not of two distinct items, but of a loving awareness, or a discerning love, we can begin to do justice to Butler's phraseology. When these minimum conditions are fulfilled, we may say that there is 'love (or hatred) of the value-bearing'. (If a man loves a woman who, unknown to him, is a forger, he loves a dishonest person. But it would seem misleading to name his condition 'love of what is dishonest', for that would suggest that dishonesty was one of the qualities towards which his love was directed. On this analogy, we may properly use such a phrase as 'love of what is value-bearing' to imply that discernment of the value-bearing quality is part of the state of love.)

But this minimum does not seem enough to constitute an act of conscience in Butler's sense. For love of the value-bearing is only a special case of what Butler calls a particular passion or affection. The qualities which excite a passion may or may not be value-bearing, and when the passion-exciting qualities are also value-bearing, the passion may be a love of the good or hatred of the bad; but it may, on the other hand, be hatred of the good or love of the bad. We are assuming that, if the minimum conditions are fulfilled, there is loving awareness of value-bearing qualities which bear a positive value, and loathing awareness of value-bearing qualities which bear a negative value. So some passions, though not all, would fulfil these minimum conditions. Let us suppose a man gives alms for the relief of a sick person. This act might be a mere case of benevolence, and no more: or it might have the seal of conscience upon it. The relief of distress is probably, under some

§ 2 · MEANING OF "CONSCIENCE"

of its forms, a value-bearing quality. The benevolent man, then, is discerning a value-bearing quality and being inclined towards it. He is fulfilling the minimum conditions of an act of conscience. But a benevolent act might lack the authority of conscience; either because it had not become subject to conscientious reflection at all, or because it was a case of misdirected benevolence, and so condemned by conscience.

The loving awareness of what is value-bearing may, therefore, be a necessary part of an act of conscience, in Butler's sense, but it cannot be the whole. There must be some feature of the act of conscience which marks it off from passions in general – that feature on account of which, if conscience and passion conflict, conscience is "supreme" and authoritative. We may express the same point by saying that a man whose conscience directs a certain course of action, has, not merely a reason for that course, but a decisive reason. Even more, he has a prepotent reason – that is, a reason of such a nature that it outweighs all contrary reasons, not merely in this instance, but on every occasion when a reason of that nature is present. A decisive reason is like a card which takes a trick in a card game: but a prepotent reason is like the ace of trumps, which must take any trick in which it is played.

§ 3 · *The meaning of 'a reason for an action'*

WHEN we speak of a man having a reason for a certain action, we do not imply that he does the action – he may have a stronger reason to the contrary. But when we say that one reason is decisive, and outweighs all others, even then we do not imply that that reason is acted on. We might express the same point by saying that, if the strongest motive is by definition the motive which issues in action, the weightiest reason does not always coincide with the strongest motive.

That men should have reasons, perhaps strong reasons, perhaps even decisive reasons for a course of action, yet not act on them, is nothing uncommon. For example, most property-owners are unwilling to lose the value of their property by fire, and all buildings are subject to some risk of fire. Most property owners, then, have a reason for taking out fire insurance policies. But some do not do so.

There are at least two possible cases of not doing what one has a reason for doing. A man may have a stronger reason for doing something different, or, although he has no stronger contrary reason, he may omit what he has a reason for doing, from inertia, perhaps, or indecision. In this latter case, we commonly speak of a man as acting unreasonably, or irrationally. A house-owner may argue that the risk of his property being destroyed by fire is small, insurance policies are expensive, and he can only pay the premiums by forgoing something else, for instance, the best education for his children: he concludes that the small risk of loss by fire is worth running. He acts not unreasonably. Another may recognise that the fire risk is substantial, and that the insurance premiums are well within his means; yet, perhaps from some neurotic fear of money commitments, he puts off taking out a policy from day to day, and year to year. That is irrational.

There are, of course, many cases in which a man has strong reasons both for and against a course of action. We may then admit that, whichever way he decides, his choice is reasonable – because one choice is reasonable it does not always follow that a contrary choice would be unreasonable, or even less reasonable. The imaginary house-owner who balanced insurance premiums against school fees might well be held to act reasonably whichever way he chose.

Any quality whatever of a possible state of affairs might afford someone a reason for promoting or averting that state of affairs – if, but only if, he were already disposed to seek or avoid that quality. It seems obvious to us that the risk of fire is a reason for taking out an insurance policy, because we assume that men wish to avoid heavy financial loss. If we are asked for reasons for avoiding war, we cite the bloodshed, suffering, and widespread insecurity which all wars produce. But for someone who has no distaste for bloodshed and suffer-

§ 3 · 'A REASON FOR AN ACTION'

ing they are not reasons at all. When we discuss the reasons for and against possible courses of action, we enumerate qualities which we expect to belong to their consequences and we treat that as a sufficient account of the reasons. We do not usually trouble to mention our assumption that one set of qualities attracts, another repels. A moment's reflection shows that our common manner of expressing ourselves is elliptical, and only works tolerably well in so far as it can be assumed that all those whom we are addressing have much the same preferences and aversions. Any difference of preferences and aversions between two people implies that some quality which, for one of them, is a reason for a certain course of action, is for the other either no reason or a reason for a contrary course of action. The very same proposals, in a party's election programme, which in one man's eyes constitute a reason for supporting the party, will give an elector of another disposition a reason for voting against it.

As we have seen, there are cases in which a man has reasons both for and against a course of action, and it is impossible to say that a decision either way would be unreasonable, or even that it would be less reasonable than a decision the other way. There are other cases in which, of two possible decisions, we might say that though both are reasonable one is more reasonable than the other: and others again in which one decision is reasonable and another unreasonable. We know that men often make the less reasonable, or an unreasonable choice – choices for which they have weak reasons or no reasons. In short, one is tempted to say, strong passions may get the better of weighty reasons. Yet the reasons are themselves derived from preferences and aversions, that is, from passions. Thus in order to give a meaning to the 'weight' of a reason we must consider at the same time what is meant by the 'strength' of a passion.

Butler recognises, and often mentions, a distinction between the "strength" of internal "principles" and their degree of authority – one being "superior", another "inferior". "The principle of reflection or conscience being compared with the

[79]

CH. 3 · CONSCIENCE

various appetites, passions, and affections in men, the former is manifestly superior and chief, without regard to strength ... Had it strength as it has right ... it would absolutely govern the world" (*S*. 2.13, 14). "Man may act according to that principle or inclination which for the present happens to be strongest. ... Suppose a man, foreseeing the ... danger of certain ruin, should rush into it for the sake of a present gratification, he in this instance would follow his strongest desire" (*S*. 2.10). Butler seems to imply that the strongest "principle" is, by definition, that which issues in action. This is a natural and usual interpretation of the notion of strength. But it is not its only possible interpretation.

We can, by introspection, compare the felt strengths of different passions. And strength in this sense must be different from that in which the action-prompting principle is, as such, the strongest. For we may make the comparison when we do not yet know how we are going to act, or when none of the passions or other "principles" we are contemplating can be acted on at all. A man in a prison cell can compare with one another, not only the relative strength of his desire to attempt escape by an attack on his warder, and his desire to eat his supper and go to sleep; he may also compare the relative strength of his desires for a box at the opera and a dinner at the Ritz, though both objectives are hopelessly out of reach. We may use the name 'felt strength' for what is compared in this introspective way. Strength in the sense in which an action-prompting principle is, as such, the strongest, may be called 'effective strength'.

Passions may vary, not only in felt strength and effective strength, but in persistence. If impulses of a particular type – 'occurrent passions' – are felt repeatedly, they constitute what we have called a 'continuant passion'. A continuant passion may be weak or strong. It may be persistent, yet usually overruled by other passions. In proportion as it is not only persistent but effective, it may be said to have 'continuing strength'.

A man's actions are not always prompted by occurrent

passions. Many are the results of planning, and tend towards the comparatively remote realisation of the objective of some continuant passion. An ambitious man may make a speech at a political meeting at the prompting of an occurrent fame-seeking impulse – an occurrent passion of the ambitious type. But he may make his speech as part of an ambitious campaign, which only the thought of substantial fame and power to be achieved at some remoter time makes worth while. Or the two motives might, of course, mingle.

Men's passions conflict with one another. In every man, by definition, the conflict is resolved when an action is prompted by the passion which has most effective or continuing strength. Thus the difference between reasonable and unreasonable conduct cannot lie in the operation or failure to operate of the strongest passion, in this sense of 'strong': for if it did all conduct would be reasonable.

It is possible that the passion with greatest felt strength does not always carry the day. This is perhaps what some writers imply when they use William James' well known phrase "action in the line of greatest resistance". But it would not be plausible to suggest that an action is reasonable when it is prompted by the passion with greatest felt strength. For that would imply that there is no greater likelihood of determining one's actions reasonably "in a cool hour", when the felt strength of all passions is low, than at other times.

A man does not act reasonably if he habitually yields to strongly felt occurrent passions, disregarding all persistent passions with remoter objectives. Nor does he act reasonably if he "never *is*, but always *to be* blest" – if, that is, he spends all his energies on planning for remote, perhaps unattainable, objectives, to the neglect of many which are attainable. He acts reasonably when he achieves some kind of harmony or balance of nearer and remoter objectives, not inhibiting all occurrent impulses uncritically, but not permitting them to frustrate settled plans or upset well tested habits: and not committing himself to remote objectives uncritically, but forgoing them if they require the enslavement of his daily and hourly impulses during an indefinite time, for an uncertain gain. We may follow Aristotle in supposing that this balance cannot be defined in a general formula, but can only be discerned, by a man of good judgement, in concrete cases. The achieving of such a balance is the work of Butler's "cool self-love".

We have said that, whenever a man finds certain qualities attractive or repulsive, it follows that he has a reason for promoting or averting them: that, in brief, every passion, as such, constitutes a reason. Moreover, in a sense the stronger the passion – in any of the senses of 'strong' already noticed – the stronger the reason. For the stronger the passion, the more difficult it will be to achieve a harmony in which that passion is frustrated, the stronger, therefore, the presumption that it must have some place in the scheme. But some passions are more refractory to harmonisation than others. To take an extreme example, a man may have a disastrous passion, such as a passion for taking extravagant risks (like James Pethel, one of Max Beerbohm's *Seven men*). The only alternatives may be to sacrifice this passion and to sacrifice most of the rest. Even if a passion constitutes a strong reason for acting in a particular way, it may well not constitute a decisive reason, and we cannot say that the strongest passion – in any sense of 'strong' – is, as such, a decisive reason. As far as we can see at present, a decisive reason can only be found by the informal deliberative process of harmonising and balancing. Here is one of Butler's descriptions of the process. "If the generality of mankind were to cultivate within themselves the principle of self-love; if they were to accustom themselves often to set down and consider what was the greatest happiness they were capable of attaining for themselves in this life, and if self-love were so strong and prevalent as that they would uniformly pursue this their supposed chief temporal good, without being diverted from it by any particular passion; it would manifestly prevent numberless follies and vices ... It is indeed by no means the religious or even moral institution of life." But

§ 3 · 'A REASON FOR AN ACTION'

certainly self-love is "a much better guide than passion, which has absolutely no bound nor measure but what is set to it by this self-love, or moral considerations" (*Pr.* 41). The implied opposition, in this passage, between self-love and the passions is corrected elsewhere, for example in *S.* 11.9, where Butler writes "happiness or satisfaction consists only in the enjoyment of those objects which are by nature suited to our several particular appetites, passions, and affections".

These passages remind us that self-love and moral considerations are distinct, and that when conscience comes into play it affords a reason for action of a unique kind – a prepotent reason. We laid down, as the minimum characteristics of an act of conscience, (1) awareness of a value-bearing quality, and (2) inclination towards or away from the subject of the value-bearing quality – or, more briefly, a loving awareness, or a discerning love. But the prepotency cannot lie in the preponderant strength of the inclination. For conscience would then not constitute a stronger reason than a strong passion would. And Butler assumes that conscience may not be strong at all. Nor can the prepotency lie in any tendency to produce a harmony or balance among the passions. For conscience would then be indistinguishable from self-love.

The minimum characteristics of an act of conscience are therefore not enough. When a man judges conscientiously, it is not enough that he should be aware of a quality which is in fact value-bearing, and feel an inclination, for both these conditions might be satisfied by some state different from an act of conscience. The prepotent reason for acting, which conscience alone affords, must lie in some further awareness or responsiveness.

Whenever a man forms a conscientious judgement about a particular action, past or projected, there is a certain truth about that action of the kind we have called a 'moral singular', to the effect that that action was, or would be if it occurred, right, or good, or wrong, or bad. The perception of this moral singular may be what Butler means by the "authority" of conscience. Or we may take the view that authority is a distinct

[83]

moral quality *sui generis*, belonging to certain inclinations, and that an act of conscience includes the perception of this quality. Whichever alternative we choose, the further consequences are much the same.

We need not confine the notion of conscience to the judging of particular actions or situations. It will also include the acknowledgement of moral universals. But for simplicity we may consider the limited case, in which conscience is concerned with particulars. Let us suppose, then, that the defining characteristics of an act of conscience are (1) awareness of a value-bearing quality, as belonging to a certain subject; (2) perception of a moral singular, to the effect that that subject has a certain moral quality; (3) inclination towards, or away from, that subject – according as its moral quality is positive or negative. We will add, as before, that these elements are to be regarded as forming a unity, so that it would be more appropriate to speak of 'loving awareness, or discerning love, of what is value-bearing, and of its value'. It has already been assumed that, whenever anything has a moral quality, it also has a value-bearing quality, which is universally connected with that moral quality: this assumption we named 'uniformity of duty' or 'uniformity of values'. It is the assumption that every moral singular would be deducible from a moral universal, together with the fact that a certain particular has a certain value-bearing quality. So the exercise of conscience upon a particular situation might also be called 'loving awareness of an instance of a moral universal'.

In the exercise of conscience a man always has a prepotent reason for the conduct which conscience enjoins. And this must be distinct from the strong or weak reasons for a course of action which he might have, in the harmonising or balancing of his passions, "were conscience out of the case". Although Butler holds that the guidance of conscience and of self-love tend to coincide (and even coincide absolutely "if we take in the future, and the whole", and God's "good and perfect administration of things" – *S.* 3.9), they are distinct, and may fail to coincide as far as this life is concerned. If we suppose

§ 3 · 'A REASON FOR AN ACTION'

that in any instance a man's self-love points, or seems to point, to a course of action condemned by conscience, he has, necessarily and always, a decisive reason against that course of action. He may, of course, follow self-love, or "supposed self-love", none the less, just as he may act against the strongest reasons of self-love.

In general, the qualities of any state of affairs give a man a reason for pursuing or promoting it only if they are attractive to him. But moral qualities must differ in this respect from qualities in general. A moral quality, as such, constitutes a reason for acting in a certain way towards its subject – promoting it or bringing it about or averting it or diminishing it. As Butler puts it, there is a "moral fitness and unfitness of actions, prior to all will whatever": "there is in the nature of things an original standard of right and wrong" (*An.* 2.8.11).

§ 4 · *The 'intrinsic stringency' of moral qualities*

SUPPOSE a man wishes to know what reason there is for an action, he often asks questions of the form 'why should I do so and so?' This expression is a standard formula for casting doubt on the existence of reasons for an action. If a man said 'why should I try to avert war?' we might reply by pointing out that all wars produce much suffering. He might then say, without any absurdity, 'I know that if war were averted much suffering would be prevented, but why should I seek to prevent suffering?' But it would be absurd to say 'I know that it's right to prevent war, but why should I do what's right?' The absurdity consists of simultaneously giving a reason and doubting whether there is a reason. The giving of a reason for an action may be compared with the giving of a reason for a belief.

It is not absurd to say 'I know that this is a tadpole, but why should I believe that it will turn into a frog?': but it is absurd to say 'I know that this is a tadpole and that all tadpoles turn into frogs, but why should I believe that this will turn into a frog?' Here I commit the absurdity of simultaneously giving the proof of a conclusion and casting doubt on the conclusion. Acknowledging a moral quality and doubting whether there is any reason for acting in a certain way towards what possesses it is rather like giving the proof and doubting the conclusion.

The analogy is not perfect, because the ascription of a moral quality is not always a decisive reason for a course of action. We cannot simultaneously and all the time pursue all the goods there are and avoid all the evils there are: we may be faced with a choice of evils or a conflict of duties. When we say that there is always a prepotent reason for the acts enjoined by conscience, we do not mean that every moral quality constitutes a prepotent reason. But it constitutes a reason which can only be overruled by some other moral consideration. For example, it may be that I could do good by giving away the whole of my income and property as alms. It does not follow that I have a decisive reason for doing so. And to do so would certainly be contrary to self-love. But the opposition of self-love does not outweigh the goodness of unlimited alms-giving, unless self-love is backed by conscience. It might well be so backed, since by unlimited alms-giving I should incapacitate myself for all sorts of other valuable activities. In that case, one moral consideration is outweighed by another. The prepotency of the reasons given by conscience consists in the fact that they can never be outweighed by reasons of some other kind.

The analogy between reasons for an action and reasons for a belief can now be made a little closer. I might say 'I know that tadpoles turn into frogs unless they die before maturity, but why should I suppose that this tadpole will turn into a frog?' Here I am not giving a proof and doubting the conclusion: but what I say is still absurd in so far as I have given a reason, though not a conclusive reason, and implied that there is no reason at all. (I might of course claim, without absurdity, that the inconclusive reason is not sufficient.) Similarly, when I have acknowledged the rightness of averting war, it is absurd to suggest that there is no reason for averting it. But again I may suggest that the reason is not adequate. I may hold that, while it is right to avert war if possible, it is also right to defend one's country from attack, although war might be averted by surrender: and I may not admit that the former obligation is so strong as always to override the latter. Then I may hold, without absurdity, that there are not always decisive reasons for every course of action calculated to avert war; but not that there is no reason.

This development of Butler's account of conscience, which may or may not be on lines of which Butler would have approved, seems consistent with our established way of expressing ourselves. We do regard a statement of the rightness of an action or the goodness of an end as giving a reason, though not always a decisive reason, for doing the action or pursuing the end. The assumption that the presence of a moral quality is always in itself a reason for some course of action may be named 'the principle of the intrinsic stringency of moral qualities'. This is the principle that their 'stringency' is "prior to all will whatever", and does not arise from their attractiveness or unattractiveness to anyone.

Something like the principle of intrinsic stringency does seem to be implied by Butler, in so far as he regards conscience as theoretically distinct from self-love. They may practically coincide "for the most part", if we take only this life into account, and altogether, if we take into account the justice of God hereafter, and the assurance that "all shall be set right at the final distribution of things" (*S*. 3.8). But since they are distinct principles, even when they support the same course of conduct the reasons by which conscience supports it cannot be the same as those by which self-love supports it. And the reasons of conscience cannot lie in the best possible balance or harmonisation of a man's passions, for those would be the reasons of self-love. They must, then, lie in the fact that the act of conscience discloses a reason of a special kind, "prior to", and independent of, "all will whatever". If the foregoing development of Butler's views is on the right lines, the principle of intrinsic stringency seems to be a more precise and explicit statement of what Butler had in mind when he spoke of "authority".

§ 5 · *Criticism of the principle of intrinsic stringency*

THE notion of intrinsic stringency seems in some ways to fit our accepted ideas about the reasons for an action, but in some ways not. The absurdity, suggested above, of saying that an action is right or good, and denying that there is any reason for it, is a real absurdity, which anyone who attends to the meanings of the words must surely feel. But we must distinguish between the statement '*there are* reasons for acting in such and such a way' and the statement '*I have* reasons'. The statement 'such and such an action would be right or good, but *I have* no reason for doing it' is perhaps not so obviously absurd. The way in which we use such words as 'right' and 'good' is notoriously elusive. A man who made the foregoing statement might be using the word 'right' to refer to some standard of conduct to which he was uncommitted – what the world approves, perhaps, and he does not. But if he said 'this would be the best thing for me to do, but I have no reason for doing it', the absurdity would reappear.

Thus there is some support, in our common way of expressing ourselves, for the view that the ascription of a moral quality is, as such, the stating of a reason. But there is also evidence to the contrary. Suppose a man were to say 'I have a reason for doing such and such an action, but I have no inclination to do it, nor any inclination to gain anything that might be gained by doing it, or avoid anything that might be avoided by doing it'. Here again there would surely be a kind of absurdity. There is an air of contradiction about saying at the same time that an action answers to no need whatever in one's own nature and that one has a reason for it. If we acknowledge the absurdity of this sort of statement, when a man says that he has a reason he implies that he has an inclination: and if

§ 5 · INTRINSIC STRINGENCY CRITICISED

we acknowledge the absurdity of the previous combination, then when a man says that an act is right or good he implies that he has a reason for it. It would follow that when a man calls an action right or good he implies that he is inclined towards it (either on its own account or on account of its consequences). He may of course also, on other grounds, be inclined against it.

In so far as a man's conscience approves an action, he must be to a certain extent inclined towards it: that follows from the definition of conscience which Butler's language seemed to imply. But we saw that, in order to distinguish conscience from self-love, we had to include in it recognition of, or responsiveness to a moral quality. The authority of conscience lies in the intrinsic stringency of the moral quality. The possession of a moral quality by an action must constitute, on this view, a reason for or against the action, quite without reference to any inclination towards or away from the action which someone may have.

Thus, the notion of intrinsic stringency seems only partly consistent with our common assumptions. It requires us to recognise a unique kind of reason for acting, not connected with human desires as all other reasons are. It does not follow that Butler's theory of conscience, or the Butlerian theory as we have developed it, is false. We may be willing to believe that there is something unique about moral thinking, and that close analogies between moral thinking, and the objects and notions with which it is concerned, on the one hand, and on the other all the rest of our thinking, are not to be expected.

Many modern philosophers would hold that such notions as intrinsic stringency are produced by a confused objectification of our own feelings and attitudes: we are deluded, they would say, by the old and well known wish to find a substance for every substantive and a quality for every adjective. They would interpret the connections we have seen between rightness or goodness, and reasons and inclinations, on some such lines as these. When people use words, they are not only making descriptive statements, but are also manifesting their own feelings, attitudes, and habits. A man who uses such words as 'right' and 'good' may be describing something, and indicating qualities of it by these words. But he is also manifesting his own favourable attitude to what he describes. To manifest an attitude is not to describe it. It may be manifested by actions, tones of voice, expressions of face, or gestures, as well as by words: but it can't be described by those means. If a man is offered a bribe, and says 'no, it would be wrong for me to accept', by his use of the word 'wrong' he reveals something about his own character or mood, of much the same kind as what he might have revealed by recoiling with a look of horror. If a man said 'this would be the best thing for me to do, but I've no reason for doing it', he would not be contradicting himself. But he would be saying something strange and absurd, because there would be a conflict between his assertion and his behaviour. He would be denying that the action answered to any inclination in him while at the same time displaying the inclination. He would be rather like a man saying, in harsh and aggressive tones, 'I'm not in the least angry', or writing, while very drunk, the words 'my hand is perfectly steady'.

If we assume that statements containing such words as 'right' and 'good' have, as their sole function, to name qualities which actions or ends might have, and we then notice that such statements also give reasons for actions, we easily reach the conclusion that the qualities named are of a peculiar kind, and have the peculiar property of intrinsic stringency. But we need not make that assumption. It is sufficient to suppose that by such statements we draw attention to familiar and unmysterious qualities, like happiness or suffering, harmony or discord, love or hate, and manifest the attraction or repugnance inspired in us by those qualities. A man who ascribes rightness or goodness to anything, sincerely and unironically, is always giving a reason because he is always manifesting an inclination.

Theories on these lines can be made very plausible, and have been worked out in detail by a number of writers, notably Mr C. L. Stevenson, in his book *Ethics and language*. What

§ 5 · INTRINSIC STRINGENCY CRITICISED

makes them plausible is the fact that when concrete examples of ethical statements are carefully and patiently examined, and interpreted as describing the non-moral qualities of things and displaying someone's favourable or unfavourable attitude to the things which have the qualities, the individual interpretations seem plausible on their own merits.

But there is no ground for preferring what, for the moment, may be called 'attitude' theories to theories, such as Butler's, which give moral qualities a unique status in the world, unless we are already making some assumption as to the type of theory which is acceptable. The attitude theories will appeal to those who accept the principle of Occam's razor, that we should use as few distinct kinds of concept as possible in our general account of the world. This is not the place to discuss the principle of conceptual economy on its own merits. It is enough for us to note that it is not self-evident, and may be rejected, and that we are still free to look at such a moral philosophy as Butler's on its own merits. We cannot do so unless we make *some* kind of assumption about what makes a theory acceptable. But the only assumptions we need make are two. (1) That a theory shall not be self-contradictory; (2) that it shall not be utterly at variance with all our accustomed moral thinking. The second principle cannot safely be made stricter. For our accustomed moral thinking may well be confused and inconsistent. Part of the task of moral philosophy is to remove those faults. The most we can ask is that it shall give our accustomed thinking what weight it can, without sacrificing clarity or consistency.

§ 6 · *Uniformity of conscience and uniformity of duty restated*

IN the first section of this chapter we said that it was hardly possible to deny the existence of diversity of conscience – and very substantial and widespread diversity. We accepted the evolutionary view of human nature of which Butler took no account. But in subsequent sections, in order not to multiply

CH. 3 · CONSCIENCE

qualifying clauses, we gave an analysis of the notion of conscience which was inconsistent with the existence of diversity. That analysis was summarised in the phrase 'loving awareness of what is value-bearing, and of its value'. If we assume, with Butler, the uniformity of value, it follows that consciences must be uniform; that is, that if someone is lovingly aware of the value of a certain object, then if anyone else contemplating the same object is not lovingly aware of its value, his state is not an act of conscience. The analysis must now be amended, so that it will be significant to speak of differences of conscience.

In modern usage, the word 'conscience' is not consistently applied. Sometimes we follow Kant's dictum, that an erring conscience is a chimera, and if a man makes what we consider misguided moral judgements we say that he has failed to search his conscience, or is not allowing his conscience to make its voice heard, or something of that kind. More often, probably, we allow that the deliverances of conscience may differ, and we are inclined to use the name as almost a synonym for what some writers have called the "tribal self" or the "super-ego" or the "ego-ideal". And sometimes we compromise, and speak of a relatively unenlightened or uninstructed conscience.

When 'conscience' means, as it has meant in our analysis so far, a power of responding rightly to the values which things actually have, we may use the nickname 'Kantian conscience'. But there might, of course, be such a thing as an illusory Kantian conscience: a man might respond lovingly to something as having a value which in fact it lacks. If we stress the intellectual part of the process, he will be mistakenly believing a false moral universal or moral singular; he will be believing that something bad is good, or that something good is bad, or some right action is wrong, or some wrong action right. We may give the nickname 'Freudian conscience' to the power of responding, rightly or wrongly, to things as having values which they may or may not have. Kantian consciences will be a subclass of Freudian consciences: a Freudian conscience will be either a real or an illusory Kantian conscience.

§ 6 · UNIFORMITY OF CONSCIENCE AND OF DUTY

In asserting the diversity of conscience we are asserting the diversity of Freudian consciences; it follows, given the uniformity of duty, that there are illusory Kantian consciences – in other words, that men's consciences can guide them aright but have sometimes guided them wrongly. But if we modify Butler's teaching by admitting diversity of conscience on evolutionary grounds, we may also suppose that man's moral knowledge is capable of development. We need not consign all but a small enlightened part of mankind to a limbo for the morally blind. There may surely be different degrees of moral enlightenment. It will follow that we must revise the too sharply defined deductions which were suggested at the beginning of this chapter. It was said that, if we denied uniformity of conscience, we must also give up either the uniformity of duty or the authority of conscience. But we need not do so without qualification.

The first geometers assumed implicitly that there was a single true system of geometry, the Euclidean, and that the facts of the physical world must conform to it. This opinion prevailed up to quite recent times, and it seemed to Kant that one of the chief problems of philosophy was to understand how we could know the geometrical properties of the world independently of experience. We now know that there can be alternative geometries, derived from different sets of postulates, and that the question how far one or another of them is applicable to the physical world can only be decided by empirical means. But because earlier geometers confused *a priori* with physical geometry, and did not notice the possibility of using alternative postulates, we do not describe their condition as one of sheer geometrical ignorance or unenlightenment. We recognise that there has been an increase in the degree of geometrical insight.

Similarly there may well be higher and lower degrees of moral insight. That need not of course imply – what modern men, in spite of so many appearances to the contrary, still so readily assume – that the development of moral notions throughout human history has consisted, and will consist, of

[93]

a steady progression from less to greater insight. All we need to assume is that all the diverse consciences of men could theoretically be ordered according to their degree of moral insight. That whatever has a certain value-bearing quality has a certain value is a universal truth, "prior to all will whatever". This principle, of the uniformity of duty or value, is unshaken. But men's apprehension of such a truth may be very confused and intermittent, or comparatively clear and steady. They may succeed in recognising it in some of its instances, while remaining blind to it in others. For example, it is, as Butler might say, "very supposable" that men should recognise the value of compassion when their friends or neighbours are concerned, but fail to recognise it, and follow some delusive principle, in dealings with strangers or enemies.

The authority of conscience, in Butler's full sense, will belong only to an enlightened conscience, conscience in the Kantian sense. For only the enlightened conscience will be responding to authentic moral truths, which have intrinsic stringency. But an unenlightened conscience will have a sort of authority. For though its attributions of value are mistaken, it follows its mistaken courses *sub specie boni*. It responds to the appearance of intrinsic stringency, though the reality is lacking. Or instead of speaking of quasi-authority we might say that authority also has degrees. The more fully and clearly a man recognises moral truths, the greater the authority of his conscience: but even a confused and partial recognition of them carries some authority.

CHAPTER 4

SELFISHNESS AND EGOISM

§ 1 · *Psychological egoism*

BUTLER'S discussions of selfishness are directed against two distinct, and incompatible, errors: one characteristic of philosophers, the other of men of the world.

He wished to give an account of human nature, and its virtuous and vicious dispositions, which would refute both the teaching of psychological egoists, such as Hobbes, who held that every action is necessarily selfish, and the assumptions of less sophisticated people, who supposed that good conduct and self-interested conduct must be antithetical, and virtue must imply self-denial. He relies on two main contentions: (1) that a correct analysis of the notion of a selfish or "interested" action shows that it applies to some actions only, not to all; (2) that it shows also that the class of actions which are good or virtuous and the class of those which are selfish or interested are not mutually exclusive, but overlap to a considerable extent.

The theory of universal selfishness, known as psychological egoism, and in one of its forms as psychological hedonism, seems to have a perennial life. It has often been refuted by philosophers, and Butler's is the classic refutation of it. Yet it flourishes still, and is felt by many people to have the force of an axiom, whose denial is absurd. There is no doubt that, as Butler made plain, its plausibility rests partly on confusions about the meaning of words. These confusions we must now try to remove.

The theory of universal selfishness seems to rest on two supports. (1) Every action of mine is prompted by motives or desires or impulses which are *my* motives, not someone else's (*Pr*. 35). This fact might also be expressed by saying

[95]

that "whenever I act I am always pursuing my own ends, or seeking to satisfy my own desires". And from this statement we might pass to the statement "I am always pursuing something for myself, or seeking my own satisfaction". Here is what seems like a proper description of a man acting selfishly, and if the description applies to all actions of all men it follows that all men in all their actions are selfish.

(2) It might be added – though Butler does not develop the point – that for this conclusion we can find some empirical evidence. There is no doubt that men sometimes act hypocritically, and affect to be disinterested when they are not. And they sometimes deceive themselves in supposing that they are disinterested. If we have some antecedent reason for believing in universal selfishness, the existence of hypocritical and self-deceived action will confirm the hypothesis. It will show that the appearance of disinterested action is reconcilable with the reality of selfish action, and will make it easier to suppose that in other cases also the appearance of disinterestedness is illusory.

But the empirical evidence is not enough to prove universal selfishness unsupported by some antecedent presumption in its favour. To Butler it seemed obvious that from principle (1) it could not follow that men always act selfishly. But it will be as well to see what sort of grounds there are for accepting principle (1), and what exactly this principle amounts to.

On the face of it, there may be exceptions to the generalisation that every action of mine is prompted by motives of mine. For example, I may be hypnotised, and perform some action at the suggestion of the hypnotist which I should never have performed unhypnotised. Let us imagine for the moment that the vulgar conception of hypnotism is true, according to which a hypnotist is a sort of magician, who by suitable spells can bind the will of others independently of any previous readiness to co-operate on their part. If that were true, we should surely have to admit that people's actions were sometimes prompted by someone else's motives or desires, not their own. We cannot be certain that such a dependence of one man's

§ 1 · PSYCHOLOGICAL EGOISM

actions on another man's will never exists, and therefore we cannot be certain that a man's actions are always, without any exception, prompted by his own desires or motives.

It may be replied that performances produced in the magically hypnotic way could not properly be called 'actions', in the sense in which moralists use the word, any more than the convulsions produced by an electric shock, or blinking in response to a dazzling light. Only what results in some way from the will or desires of the agent can be an action. If we imagine that a hypnotist might arbitrarily induce his subject to behave in ways repugnant to him when unhypnotised, there are, it might be said, two possibilities. He might generate in his subject desires or impulses never previously felt, or he might bring about bodily movements and utterances directly, as though by giving an electric shock. But if the first alternative is realised, the statement that the subject's actions are prompted by motives of his own remains true: while if the second alternative is realised, the subject's performances are not actions at all, so that the generalisation is still unaffected.

All this could be put more precisely, but enough has perhaps been said to explain the axiomatic certainty which seems to belong to the statement that a man's actions must be prompted by his own motives. When a case, real or imaginary, is produced in which it appears that a man acts from no motive or desire of his own, we may at once classify his performance as not properly an action. Alternatively, we may retain the right to call his performance an action by postulating a desire or motive on the subject's part in spite of appearances. In short, the generalisation that all my actions spring from *my* desires or motives proves to be a disguised tautology, which must be true, given the accepted meaning of the word 'action'. In an undisguised form, it would appear as the statement 'every performance which springs from a motive of mine is a performance which springs from a motive of mine'. And this tautology cannot support the conclusion that all my performances spring from selfish motives.

CH. 4 · SELFISHNESS AND EGOISM

Psychological egoists would claim that every action is prompted, not merely by a motive of the agent's own, but by a motive of a particular kind. If we use the notion of an 'objective', introduced in chapter 2, § 3, we may express their claim by saying that the objective of the action, or of the passion or desire from which it arises, is always some state of the agent himself. We can get a clear enough view of their claim if we confine our attention to the conscious motives of deliberate actions, disregarding impulsive actions and unconscious motives. It would, indeed, be open to psychological egoists to hold that, in spite of appearances, every action proceeded from wholly selfish unconscious motives. But it is hard to see how this thesis could be made plausible unless there were some grounds for a theory of universal selfishness independently of hypotheses about unconscious motives.

Suppose a man acts deliberately in pursuance of some "passion, affection, or appetite". He has an objective in view, and his thought of the objective has an attractive or repellent tone. (If he acts under the influence of fear or aversion, the repellent tone belongs to what he seeks to avoid, and the objective is the avoidance.)

We have already seen (chapter 2, § 3) that Butler overstates his case when he implies that the objective is never a state of the agent himself, but always something "external" (*Pr.* 35; *S.* 11.6, and elsewhere). Part of the reason for Butler's insistence on externality is that he assumes that, if the objective of a passion were not external, it would be a state of pleasure on the part of the agent. But this is not obviously true. Someone might aim at recovering from an illness, or becoming a good swimmer. And he might be elated by his recovery, or enjoy swimming. But the recovery and the elation, or the power to swim and the enjoyment of swimming, are distinct and separable facts about him. A man may feel no elation, in spite of his restoration to health, and may train himself in swimming for the sake of its usefulness, although immersion in water is disagreeable to him. On the face of it,

§ 1 · PSYCHOLOGICAL EGOISM

therefore, we should expect to find two distinguishable kinds of action; action aiming at some state of the agent himself, whether or not that state will be pleasant, and action aiming at a pleasant state of the agent himself. Similarly there might be actions aiming at avoiding a certain state of the agent himself, whether painful or not, and actions aiming at the avoidance of a painful state.

Let us suppose, with common sense, but against psychological egoists like Hobbes, that sometimes the objective of an action is not a state of the agent himself. Then again, on the face of it, there will be two distinguishable kinds of action; those which aim at some state of affairs, whether or not it will be pleasant to the agent, and those aiming at some state of affairs pleasant to the agent. And there would be a similar distinction between actions aiming at avoidance of something. For example, a man might try to save someone else from drowning, and he might or might not feel sorrow at the victim's death, if he were unsuccessful, or joy at the rescued man's safety. We should expect to find two kinds of action; action aiming simply at saving the drowning man's life, without reference to any feelings which his death or safety will cause the rescuer to have, and action aiming at the joy of knowing the man was saved, or at avoiding the grief of knowing he was drowned: though the boundary might be hard to draw.

Psychological egoism is sometimes expressed in a hedonistic form, to the effect that 'the motive of a man's action is always his own pleasure (or pain)'. We can see now that this statement might have at least two meanings. When a man acts deliberately and purposively, he surveys future happenings which his conduct might influence or bring about. The possibilities he contemplates have an attractive or repellent tone in various degrees. It is sometimes supposed that he always chooses whatever has the most attractive, or at any rate the least repellent, tone. When he does so, it is consistent with ordinary language to say that 'he aims at what is pleasant to him, or what pleases him, or at avoiding what is unpleasant

CH. 4 · SELFISHNESS AND EGOISM

to him'. But by this description another meaning is suggested; namely, that he aims at some state of affairs which will give him pleasure when it comes about, or which he believes will give him pleasure. Now it may often be true that a possibility which has an attractive tone will, when it is realised, in fact give pleasure; and it may often be true that the man who contemplates it believes that when realised it will give him pleasure. But there seems to be no reason why either of these propositions should be universally true. Men are notoriously sometimes disappointed when they get what they have ardently desired; and it seems quite possible that a contemplated future happening should be attractive, although there is no distinct belief about the pleasure it will cause. In any case, the attractive tone of the contemplated possibility, the pleasure produced by its realisation, and the expectation of pleasure from its realisation, are three distinct facts. It would therefore be illegitimate for psychological hedonists to pass from the premiss that a man always aims at what pleases him – that is, at the possibility which has the most attractive or least repulsive tone – to the conclusion that a man always aims at whatever will give him most pleasure, or least pain, when it happens; or at whatever he thinks will give him most pleasure or least pain. Such a deduction would only seem to be possible through confusion of the various senses of such expressions as 'what pleases him', or 'what gives him pleasure'.

It was supposed just now, as the premiss from which psychological hedonists might reach their confused conclusion, that a man always chooses whatever has the most attractive, or at any rate the least repellent, tone. But that is doubtful. Even if men very often choose in the way described, it is well known that they sometimes act, as William James put it, in the "line of greatest resistance". There cannot be deliberate action without contemplation of future possibilities: for that is part of what we mean by 'deliberate'. But perhaps men sometimes act deliberately, although none of the possibilities they foresee has any tone at all; and perhaps they sometimes aim at what has not got the most attractive tone, or at avoiding

§ 1 · PSYCHOLOGICAL EGOISM

what has not got the most repulsive tone. That they sometimes do so seems to be implied by the fact that men sometimes act on principle, or from a sense of duty, against almost overwhelming inclination. Thus the confused conclusion of psychological hedonism seems to be reached from a false premiss.

We may now consider whether psychological egoism can possibly be made plausible in its general form, in which it asserts that a man always aims at some state of himself; whether or not that state is pleasant, or conceived as pleasant, or pain-avoiding, or conceived as pain-avoiding. To make their claim plausible, egoists must make use of the well-known and important distinction between nearer and remoter aims. A man may learn to swim without any ulterior aim, desiring the ability for its own sake: or he may learn to swim so as not to feel inferior to swimmers, or so as to be able to save life. Or all these aims, and others too, may be combined.

According to the analysis suggested in chapter 2, § 3, this means that he believes, with or without good grounds, that practice in swimming tends to produce certain results; and anything which weakens his belief about the results tends to break off, or modify, his efforts to learn to swim. Let us suppose that life-saving was his sole motive for learning to swim. Then if he came to think that he was never going to need the ability to save himself or others from drowning – if, for instance, it appeared that the rest of his life would be spent far from all deep water – he would drop his swimming lessons. If he did not do so, it would follow that life-saving was not his sole motive. It is clear that, in this connection, the word 'motive' can be defined in terms of objectives. Suppose a man learns to swim, both for the sake of swimming and for the sake of life-saving. The power to swim is a nearer and the saving of life a remoter objective, in the sense that the power to swim is a contribution to the saving of life, and not *vice versa*. We commonly assume that some ends are sought for their own sake only, some as means only, and some both for their own sake and as means to something else sought for its own sake. This common assumption can be expressed in terms of our analysis

CH. 4 · SELFISHNESS AND EGOISM

as follows. A man believes that, in conjunction with permanent conditions, action A will produce effect E_1, E_1 will produce E_2, and E_1 and E_2 will produce E_3. If he comes to think that E_3 will, after all, not be produced by E_1 and E_2, he does not modify his course of action. If he comes to think that, after all, E_2 will not be produced, but E_3 will, he does not modify his course of action. But if he comes to think that neither E_2 nor E_3 will be produced, he ceases to act in ways calculated to produce E_1. He does not look beyond E_3: that is, whatever effects he may foresee from E_3, if he ceased to expect them he would not modify his conduct. All this may be more briefly expressed by saying that he seeks E_1 only as a means to E_2 and E_3, he seeks E_2 both for its own sake and as a means to E_3, and he seeks E_3 for its own sake alone.

In concrete terms, a man believes that if he stands for Parliament he will stand a good chance of being elected: he also believes that the activities of a Member of Parliament will be congenial to him, and will give him the opportunity of forwarding some public aim, for example the preservation of natural beauty. His immediate activities are directed to getting himself adopted as a candidate, and getting himself elected. But the adoption and the election are not worth achieving on their own account: they are only a means to the activities of a Member of Parliament to which they are supposed to lead. Now suppose the candidate came to think that his earlier picture of a Member of Parliament's position was quite mistaken: suppose he came to think that the daily round of business was not satisfying and stimulating, as he had supposed, but futile and tedious; and that a private member's opportunities of influencing legislation were negligible. He would then withdraw his candidature if, as we have imagined, the activities and opportunities of parliamentary life were his only motive. If he continued to be a candidate, we should conclude that either electioneering, or success in an election, had some value for him on its own account, or he had some other undiscovered ulterior aim. On the other hand, he might not withdraw his candidature if he found that only one part of his

§ 1 · PSYCHOLOGICAL EGOISM

picture of parliamentary life was mistaken. He might think that a humdrum daily round was worth putting up with for the sake of legislative ends to be achieved: or he might think the daily round of a Member of Parliament interesting enough to compensate for his ineffectiveness as an initiator of legislation. We are then entitled to say that parliamentary life and legislative influence are sought, each on its own account, and the first is also sought as a means to the other.

We seem here to have in outline an intelligible account of the relation between pursuing some end as a means and pursuing it for its own sake, in terms of a man's beliefs about the effects of his actions, and the tendency of changes in his beliefs to modify or not to modify his actions. It is only an outline, because human motives may be very complicated, and it may be hard to diagnose, in individual cases, just how far a given consequence is sought as a means, or sought for its own sake, or not sought at all (*Pr. 36*). But we can probably see the strength and weakness of psychological egoism clearly enough with the help of a somewhat schematic picture of human motives.

When some consequence is sought for its own sake alone, we may call it an 'ultimate' aim; and when it is sought partly for its own sake and partly as a means we may call it a 'subultimate' aim. When it is sought only as a means, it may be called a 'subordinate' aim.

It seems clear, in the first place, that psychological egoism could not possibly be a plausible account of subordinate aims. I light a fire in the morning in order to have a warm room in the afternoon. That the fire shall burn from the morning to the afternoon is certainly one of my aims, and by no conceivable sleight of hand can what I aim at here be made to appear as a state of myself. And no intelligent psychological egoist would attempt such a sleight of hand. But it might be maintained that all subordinate aims are sought as means to states of myself, and that all my ultimate and subultimate aims must be states of myself. This is the characteristic thesis of psychological egoism.

CH. 4 · SELFISHNESS AND EGOISM

It is certainly contrary to common sense. The common view would be that a man may have altruistic or public-spirited aims, and that these are different from private aims. A man may aim at a good education for his children, or at the enjoyment of the countryside by people at large; and again, a malevolent man may aim at the ruin of his enemies, or even the destruction of the human race. In none of those cases is a man aiming at a state of himself.

A psychological egoist would reply that these descriptions of a man's aims are abbreviated, and that it would be more accurate to say that a man aims at knowing that his children are having a good education, or at enjoying the contemplation of his enemies' ruin. But there are considerable difficulties about applying this formula to all aims. In the first place, it would imply that a man can never properly be said to have the same aims for someone else as he has for himself: he might aim at good health on his own part, for its own sake, but he could never aim at someone else's good health for its own sake. This is, at any rate, contrary to what we commonly assume, when we speak of disinterested benevolence. Secondly, if we accepted this formula, action for very remote ends would be hard to understand. For example, a man may dispose of his property by will for several generations ahead, acting, as we should commonly say, in the interests, or what he supposes to be the interests, of his remote descendants. According to egoism, what he is pursuing for its own sake must be, not the results of his will, but his own prevision of them – or possibly his own contemplation of them after death. Thirdly, the theory seems to require us to hold that a man may find sources of satisfaction and dissatisfaction in objects which, at the same time, are of no importance to him. A so-called benevolent or altruistic person might regulate a great deal of his conduct with a view to the effects other people's welfare would produce in him – sympathetic enjoyments and distresses, presumably – yet these effects are produced in him by something which he could never possibly aim at on its own account. This seems, to say the least, surprising.

§ 2 · *The meaning of "interested action"*

IN Butler's attack on the egoist doctrine, he states it as the doctrine that there can be no such thing as "disinterested" action. And he gives a somewhat unexpected account of what is meant by "interested" and "disinterested". He would object, for instance, to the phrase "disinterested benevolence", used in the previous paragraph, because it suggests that, while benevolence is disinterested, malice is not, and that the disinterestedness of a passion or way of acting is a mark of its virtuous tendency (*Pr.* 35–42; *S.* 11.5–18). In Butler's view, in the only useful sense which can be given to the word "interested", actions done from self-love are interested, and actions done from particular passions, including benevolence, are disinterested. If we called a man's actions interested whenever they arose from "a desire, or choice, or preference of his own", we should have to call all actions interested, and the word would cease to be of any use for distinguishing one class of actions from another. The goodness and badness of actions is independent of their interestedness. Good actions may be done from self-love, and may therefore be interested. Very bad actions may be done from particular passions, and so be disinterested. What could be more detestable than disinterested cruelty?

This seems rather too simple. When we contrast disinterested benevolence, or advice, or public service, with some other variety, we surely express a real distinction. A man who advises you to invest money in an undertaking from which he hopes to make a profit is not giving disinterested advice. But he is not therefore acting from self-love in Butler's refined sense. He is acting from avarice – a particular passion. Butler's enlightened self-love would prevent him from pursuing wealth uncritically and unreservedly: he would have to reconcile his avarice with his friendlier and kindlier feelings, his need for other men's trust and respect, and so on, and the outcome no doubt would be that he would not advise you to

CH. 4 · SELFISHNESS AND EGOISM

invest in his enterprise without pointing out to you at the same time his own reasons for wishing the advice to be accepted.

At this point we might invoke a distinction which Butler draws, without making much use of it, between "public" and "private" passions (*S*. 1.7, *S*. 5). The former "contribute to public good", the latter to the agent's own good. If we can accept this as a clear distinction – though it needs fuller analysis – we may suggest that an interested action is an action resulting, either from self-love, or from a private passion, such as avarice; while a disinterested action proceeds from a public passion. (Of course, in an obvious sense, a private passion might not contribute to the agent's good at all, since it might be contrary to self-love.) In discussing the distinction between interested and disinterested, Butler does not mention conscientious action. An action done at the prompting of conscience must surely also count as disinterested.

Butler's discussion of disinterestedness presupposes his view that "particular affections rest in the external things themselves", which we have already seen reason to criticise (chapter 2, § 3). In the light of those criticisms, we may restate his position in a modified form, as follows.

Among the objectives of men's desires and actions are (1) future states of themselves, (2) future facts or happenings other than states of themselves. Some actions are not inspired directly by the desire for an objective of either of these kinds, but by the general desire for one's own happiness (self-love), or by reflective approval and disapproval (conscience). Interested actions are those which proceed from desires of the first type, or from self-love: others are disinterested. Since the course of conduct required by self-love coincides very largely, if not entirely, with the course of conduct required by conscience, it follows that the same course of action may be, in one instance, interested, and in another not.

But to give a fuller analysis of the difference between interested and disinterested action we must refer to the distinction between ultimate, subultimate, and subordinate objectives.

§ 2 · MEANING OF "INTERESTED ACTION"

A man would not be acting disinterestedly if he gave advice – even good advice – for the ultimate objective of his own profit. If the advantage of the person advised were a subultimate objective, the advice would be partly disinterested and partly not.

There is a further distinction between objectives, in the degree of importance which the agent attaches to them. As we should commonly phrase it, a man who gave good advice might have as his chief aim the advantage of the person advised, but he might also foresee some gain for himself if the advice were taken, and he might regard that as an incidental good to be realised. In that case, the subultimate objective would be more important than the ultimate objective. The importance of an objective cannot be assessed by the same means as its ultimacy or subordination. The obvious measure of it is the amount of trouble a man is prepared to go to for the sake of a given end. A man abandons or modifies a purposive course of action, not only because he comes to think that it won't lead to the expected result, but also, in other cases, because he comes to think that the achievement of his purpose is going to be slower and more laborious than he had supposed, or more unfavourable to his other purposes. Let us suppose that a man stands aside from candidature for some office, in order to make way for a friend whom he believes to be better qualified. Very likely he is not unmindful of the prospect of being praised and admired for his magnanimity. But it is quite supposable that he would go to a good deal of trouble, if necessary, to procure his friend's election, while he would go to very little trouble to win a reputation for magnanimity, independently of any other objective. In that case, his subultimate objective is a good deal more important than his ultimate objective.

In such a case, if the most important objective were some future possibility other than a state of the agent, we might well say that the action was substantially disinterested, even though there were also objectives of minor importance which were future states of the agent.

CH. 4 · SELFISHNESS AND EGOISM

For present purposes, we will give the name 'motive' to any of the four sources of action which were listed above. There will be two kinds of interested motive, that is, of motives leading to interested action, and two disinterested. The moral value of an action, in Butler's view, has no connection with its interestedness or disinterestedness. It depends on "what becomes such creatures as we are, what the state of the case requires" (*Pr.* 39). Moral value can, of course, belong to intentions (*D. on V.* 2) as well as actions. But "the intention" means the agent's preconception of the future facts and happenings to be produced by his action: it does not mean his motive. Any of the motives we have listed might result in good intentions being formed.

The fourfold division of motives is not quite an accurate representation of Butler's view. For it suggests that conscience or reflection is an alternative motive, which might operate in the absence of the others. It is not certain that, in Butler's view, it would never operate in that way. But the characteristic operation of conscience is supposed to consist of reflection upon *other* motives, and the actions to which they would lead. "The mind can take a view of what passes within itself, its propensions, aversions, passions, affections, as respecting such objects, and in such degrees; and of the several actions consequent thereupon. In this survey it approves of one, disapproves of another, and towards a third is affected in neither of these ways, but is quite indifferent" (*S.* 1.8). And the characteristic operation of self-love would consist of reflection upon motives of the first two kinds.

§ 3 · *Butler on Hobbes*

PSYCHOLOGICAL egoists deny the existence of motives of the second and fourth kinds, and have to explain away the appearance of them. In various passages, Butler criticises in detail Hobbes' attempts to explain away the appearances. His treatment of Hobbes is not always quite fair, that is, he some-

§ 3 · BUTLER ON HOBBES

times derives from Hobbes' views absurdities which might easily be avoided. In *S.* 1.6, fn. he discusses the suggestion that what appears to be benevolence is really "only the love of power, and delight in the exercise of it". And in *S.* 5.1, fn. he considers Hobbes' account of sympathy and compassion. He quotes Hobbes as identifying pity with "imagination or fiction of future calamity to ourselves, proceeding from the . . . knowledge of another man's calamity". Butler remarks that such paradoxes could only come to be asserted because "this learned person had a general hypothesis, to which the appearance of good will could not otherwise be reconciled". This remark, rather than the particular refutations, really gives the essence of the matter. For the appearance of things, undistorted by theory, is that motives of all four kinds exist and sometimes issue in action: and, in particular, that men sometimes desire and seek to bring about future facts and happenings which are not states of themselves. Methods of explaining away this appearance are called for only if we already have some general reason for accepting the theory that men never seek anything but states of themselves. We have already noticed two confusions which might mistakenly be taken to support the theory. It might be supposed to follow from the proposition that the motives from which I act are always my motives. And it might be supposed to follow from the proposition that when I act deliberately I am always influenced by the attractive or repulsive tone of my thoughts about future possibilities. But we have seen that, even if both these propositions are true, the theory does not follow from them. And when this has been seen it is hard to discover any other general grounds which might support the theory.

Butler's particular refutations may therefore be considered quite briefly. Butler points out that love and exercise of power might be just as effectively manifested in doing mischief as in doing good. There might, indeed, be accidental restraints on the one kind of exercise of power. But these will not always be present. If a man could cause injury and destruction with impunity, and if he could exercise even greater power in that

CH. 4 · SELFISHNESS AND EGOISM

way than in any beneficent activity, then the very same disposition which might have led him to do good will, as a matter of course, lead him to do mischief.

The question is not about the relative strength and commonness of benevolent and malevolent desires: the question is whether benevolent desires exist at all, that is, whether there is such a thing as a desire for someone else's welfare without reference to the degree of power which would be exercised in procuring it. This is "a mere question of fact or natural history, not proveable immediately by reason". There are three methods of settling such a question. (1) Direct observation; (2) "arguing from acknowledged facts and actions"; (3) "the testimony of mankind". All these methods go to prove the existence of benevolence. The second calls for a little elucidation. "A great number of actions of the same kind, in different circumstances, and respecting different objects", Butler writes, "will prove to a certainty what principles they do not, and to the greatest probability what principles they do proceed from." We find, for instance, that a man often seems to desire some advantage for someone else, and to be pleased when he obtains it, although it was not in his own power to confer it. And we find that a man often appears to prefer to do a service to one person rather than another, although the exercise of power would be equal in either case. It is clear that what is desired in these cases cannot be the exercise of power: and it seems probable that the desire really is what it appears to be, namely a desire for someone else's welfare. The point is that, if we find, as we do, that in a great variety of cases men's desires for certain results are independent of the degree of power which would be exercised in bringing the results about, the exercise of power cannot be the ultimate objective. An advocate of the power theory might, of course, reply that men misjudge the degree to which they will be exercising power in one or another course of conduct. But to accept this perverse hypothesis we should have to suppose that they misjudge to the extent of supposing themselves to influence events which in fact they don't influence at all – as

§3 · BUTLER ON HOBBES

when a man is pleased because a friend obtains some good which he couldn't himself have conferred.

Butler's treatment of the Hobbesian theory of pity is less satisfying. He makes debating hits rather cheaply, when there was no need to do so. The theory is that, when someone else's misfortune arouses in me what are commonly regarded as sympathetic feelings, what really happens is that I am reminded of my own liability to similar ills, and so made anxious on my own account. Butler might have argued, on the same lines as before, that so called sympathetic feelings do not vary in proportion to my own liability to the misfortune I am contemplating. Other people may suffer in ways from which, by difference of character and circumstances, I am almost exempted: but this fact does not debar me from sympathising with them. He does not put the matter in this way. He points out that Hobbes has to explain why people should sympathise more with the distresses of their friends than with those of others. This, he says, in Hobbes' view must be equivalent to the question why we *fear* our friends more than others. Clearly this is an indefensible distortion, and Butler corrects it a little later. The question would really be, according to Hobbes, why "the sight of our friends in distress raises in us greater fear for ourselves than the sight of others in distress". Here Butler raises two sound objections. (1) This assertion is quite doubtful, although it is not to be doubted that most men feel more compassion for their friends than for others. But if the two assertions were identical, neither could conceivably be more doubtful than the other. (2) As soon as we ask whether the first assertion is true, and whether the second is true, it is clear that these are two distinct questions. If men feel more fear for themselves on seeing the distresses of their friends than on seeing those of others, and if they feel more compassion for their friends than for others, these are two distinct facts, and consequently "fear and compassion are not the same".

Butler is willing to recognise a grain of truth in the Hobbesian theory. Often, when we become aware of other

CH. 4 · SELFISHNESS AND EGOISM

people's misfortunes, three distinct feelings are aroused: (1) real concern; (2) some degree of satisfaction at our own freedom from the misfortune in question; (3) some reflection on our liableness to similar ill fortune. According to circumstances, one or another of these responses may be excited more strongly than the rest, or may not be excited at all. But there is no reason, because we admit the existence of the second and third, to deny the existence of the first, which alone is what is properly meant by "compassion" or "sympathy".

§ 4 · *Self-love and benevolence*

WE have already seen (chapter 2, § 2) that according to Butler there is no conflict between self-love and benevolence. Sympathetic and benevolent "affections" are as much a part of our nature as the desire for food, or riches, or rank, or fame. There are two vulgar errors in this matter. One is "that, were religion out of the case, the happiness of the present life would consist in a manner wholly in riches, honours, sensual gratifications" (*S.* 1.14). The other is that in order to be right or good our conduct must be disinterested. Butler's criticism of the second assumption is already apparent from our discussion of the notion of interestedness. Of the first, a little more may be said.

In a number of passages Butler dwells on the theme that we do not make the best provision for ourselves by attending exclusively to self-centred concerns (*Pr.* 40; *S.* 1.10 and 14; *S.* 3.7–8; *S.* 5.12; *S.* 6.10; *S.* 11; *S.* 14.9). There seem to be three points involved. (1) The most effective policy for realising such happiness as we are capable of is not to pursue happiness directly, single-mindedly, and at all times. As a matter of psychological fact, happiness is elusive: it is driven away by too eager wooing, and often comes unsought. (2) Men often give themselves up uncritically to "passions unfriendly to benevolence", on the supposition that when they are not consulting the interests of others they are necessarily

[112]

§ 4 · SELF-LOVE AND BENEVOLENCE

consulting their own. They have failed to see that particular passions may be, and that benevolence need not be, contrary to self-love. This is the typical conduct of "men of pleasure", who, as Butler sees them, ruin their health by drinking and wenching, and their estates by gaming and profusion. (3) Some of the "passions unfriendly to benevolence" are, not merely distinct from, but contrary to self-love. Such are malice, envy, revengefulness, and so on. They are "in themselves mere misery; and the satisfaction arising from the indulgence of them is little more than relief from that misery" (*S.* 3.8).

By such considerations as these, Butler supports his view that greater attention to one's own interest makes men better, not worse. All his observations seem just. But, as in other connections, he is too ready to assume uniformity. This assumption is connected with a kind of optimism characteristic of the eighteenth century. Although Butler did not expect perfection in human life, he assumed that every man was capable of such limited goodness as is open to finite creatures, and that in realising it he would also be furthering his own happiness. He left no place in his scheme for individuals less fortunately constituted, to whom the social virtues are irksome or intolerable, and who can gain such satisfactions as are open to them only through power or exploitation or contention. We can hardly avoid thinking that human nature is far more various than Butler imagined. Some men's self-love and benevolence may conspire to make them happy and virtuous, but not all are so favoured.

§ 5 · *Egoism in Butler's teaching*

A WELL-KNOWN passage in *S.* 11 has given rise to a good deal of controversy.

"Let it be allowed, though virtue or moral rectitude does indeed consist in affection to and pursuit of what is right and good as such, yet that, when we sit down in a cool hour, we can neither justify to ourselves this or any other pursuit till we are convinced that it will be for our happiness, or at least not contrary to it" (*S*. 11.20).

If this passage were an unqualified statement of Butler's own view, it would contradict other views which we have attributed to him. It was argued in chapter 3, § 4, that, according to Butler's theory of conscience, if a course of action has the moral quality of rightness or obligatoriness, that fact of itself constitutes a reason for the course of action – in the language Butler uses above, it "justifies" it to us. Yet in this passage – which is undoubtedly contrary to the tenor of his writings – he seems to imply that the prospect of my own happiness is the only possible reason for my acting in one way rather than another – or at the least a necessary condition of my having a reason.

But the inconsistency is only apparent. The eleventh *Sermon* is a piece of sustained argument against the common confusions about self-love which have already been noticed: (1) that it is in conflict with benevolence; (2) that it is in conflict with virtue; (3) that it is identical with the indulgence of a certain limited range of passions. Butler makes his purpose plain at the beginning, and his words are worth quoting in full.

"There is generally thought to be some peculiar kind of contrariety between self-love and the love of our neighbour, between the pursuit of public and of private good, insomuch that when you are recommending one of these you are supposed to be speaking against the other; and from hence arises a secret prejudice against, and frequently open scorn of, all talk of public spirit and real goodwill to our fellow-creatures." Therefore "it will be necessary to enquire what respect benevolence hath to self-love, and the pursuit of private interest to the pursuit of public, or whether there be anything of that peculiar inconsistence and contrariety between them, over and above what there is between self-love and other passions and particular affections, and their respective pursuits. . . . There shall be all possible concessions made to the favourite passion, which hath so much allowed to it, and whose cause is so uni-

§ 5 · EGOISM IN BUTLER

versally pleaded; it shall be treated with the utmost tenderness and concern for its interests" (*S.* 11.2-3).

The suspect passage, which comes nearly at the end of this sermon, is a recapitulation. Its purpose is plain. Butler claims to have shown, by arguments already discussed, that self-love requires considerable regard for others, and excludes the uncritical indulgence of "private" passions. Thus, even if – making "all possible concessions to the favourite passion" – we recognise no justification for any action except self-love, it does not follow that our conduct should be other than virtuous.

In *S.* 3.9 Butler states in its most extreme form the doctrine of the coincidence of conscience and self-love. "Conscience and self-love, if we understand our true happiness, always lead us the same way. Duty and interest are perfectly coincident: for the most part in this world, but entirely and in every instance if we take in the future and the whole; this being implied in the notion of a good and perfect administration of things." There are two distinct grounds for this claim. From a survey of human nature we reach the relatively weak conclusion that, in this life, duty and interest coincide for the most part: and from the doctrine of God's just administration we reach the stronger conclusion that in the long run – when men have come up for judgement – they will coincide entirely. If we treated the passage from *S.* 11.20 as an authoritative statement in the light of which all Butler's expressions elsewhere must be interpreted, we might conclude that the "coincidence" of self-love and conscience means that they are identical. But it has been shown that we are not entitled to use the passage in that way. And if we did we should make Butler's insistence on the "authority" and "supremacy" of conscience pointless. Butler's language is always carefully chosen. By "coincidence" he does not mean identity: the coincidence is insisted on, and is worth insisting on, just because conscience and self-love are distinct principles: the "coincidence" holds between the results of acting on them.

CHAPTER 5

THE CONTENT OF MORALITY

§ 1 · *General rules not required*

BUTLER did not think it important to look for general rules of conduct, or general formulations of right or good ends to be pursued. "The enquiries which have been made by men of leisure after some general rule, the conformity to or disagreement from which should denominate our actions good or evil, are in many respects of great service. Yet let any plain honest man, before he engages in any course of action, ask himself 'is this I am going about right, or is it wrong? is it good or is it evil?' I do not in the least doubt but that this question would be answered agreeably to truth and virtue, by almost any fair man in almost any circumstance" (*S*. 3.4).

There are three possible reasons for attaching small importance to general rules. (1) It might be said that there *are* no general rules: that every situation, and the obligations arising from it, are unique. Yet it would still be the case that, if two situations were exactly alike, in all respects which were morally relevant, the actions which ought to be done in those two situations would be the same. It might be held that in fact there never are two situations exactly alike in all moral respects. But from that supposition it would follow, not that there are no general rules, but that no general rule is applicable, in point of fact, to more than one concrete instance. It would follow that there are at least as many general moral rules as there are situations in which someone might act well or badly – that is, that they are uncountably numerous. And it would follow that general rules could not be used as premisses from which right moral judgements about particular situations could be deduced. For no one could possibly learn,

[116]

§ 1 · GENERAL RULES NOT REQUIRED

in advance of all choices, and bear in mind at all times, the uncountably numerous rules applicable to all possible situations. When people say that there are no general rules they are probably referring vaguely and inaccurately to such facts as these. (2) It might be held that, though there are general rules, which may sometimes be applicable to more than one situation, they are of little practical use, because of their large number, complexity, and so on. (3) It might be held that, though there are general rules, and though they are not impracticably numerous or complicated, they are not important in practice because we can discern the moral requirements of a given situation by attending only to that situation and what will come after it, and do not need to refer to any rule.

Butler's position is probably the third, though some things he says suggest the second. Butler would probably have held that, if general rules can be established at all, they are to be established inductively, from particular moral judgements; not that the general rules are found by some *a priori* method and the particular judgements deduced from them.

Since he does not think general rules important, Butler does not give any list of duties or virtues or vices. We have a fairly clear idea of the morality he accepted, but we draw it from what he says by way of illustration. An explicit statement might have seemed desirable if Butler had consciously questioned the assumptions of the uniformity of duty and the uniformity of conscience. But he thought that any "fair man" who reflected on a particular set of facts, without self-partiality, could reach only one conclusion as to his obligations, and could reach it without invoking a general rule.

§ 2 · *The limits of benevolence*

THERE is one proposed rule of conduct which exercised Butler's mind a good deal – the utilitarian rule that, in any situation, we should act in the way which will produce most happiness or least misery on the whole. He refers to this rule a number of times in the *Sermons*, and sometimes seems inclined to adopt it, though he never adopts it unreservedly: in the *Analogy* and the *Dissertation on virtue* he decides against it.

"The common virtues and the common vices of mankind may be traced up to benevolence, or the want of it", Butler writes in *S.* 12.31; and he goes on "leaving out the particular nature of creatures, and the particular circumstances in which they are placed, benevolence seems . . . to include in it all that is good and worthy". But he qualifies this in a footnote, where he refers to "particular obligations which we may discern and feel ourselves under, quite distinct from a perception that the observance or violation of them is for the happiness or misery of our fellow-creatures". "There are certain dispositions of mind, and certain actions", he continues, "which are in themselves approved or disapproved by mankind, abstracted from the consideration of their tendency to the happiness or misery of the world; approved or disapproved by reflection, by that principle within which is . . . the judge of right and wrong." Examples are treachery, littleness of mind, magnanimity, fidelity, honour, justice. The qualification in this footnote is insisted on much more strongly in the *Dissertation on virtue* (10). There he speaks of the "danger . . . of imagining the whole of virtue to consist in singly aiming, according to the best of their judgement, at promoting the happiness of mankind in the present state; and the whole of vice in doing what they foresee . . . is likely to produce an overbalance of unhappiness in it: than which mistakes none can be conceived more terrible. For it is certain that some of the most shocking instances of injustice, adultery, murder, perjury, and even of persecution, may, in many supposable cases, not have the appearance of being likely to produce an overbalance of misery . . . ; perhaps sometimes may have the contrary appearance."

Here two distinct questions have to be raised: what rule is to be followed, and how the rule is to be justified. Given that actions of a certain class are "vicious", acts of treachery for example, given, that is, that they are wrong in all circum-

§ 2 · LIMITS OF BENEVOLENCE

stances, their wrongness might arise from the intrinsic character of the action, or might arise from the tendency of these actions to produce certain consequences. In the terminology used in chapter 3, § 2, the value-bearing quality on which the wrongness of the action depends might be its treacherousness, that is, its relation to the present and past situation of the agent; or it might be the action's tendency to produce human misery. A utilitarian might argue that the viciousness of treachery arises solely from consequences: but that even if a given treacherous act had the appearance of producing an "overbalance of happiness" it would not therefore be right. For there are good reasons for thinking, in the first place, that most treacherous acts produce an overbalance of misery; and secondly that every treacherous act tends to weaken, both in the agent and in anyone exposed to his example, the habit of avoiding treachery. We can be more certain of these general evil tendencies of treachery than we can of the "overbalance of happiness" expected from a supposedly exceptional act of treachery. Therefore the rule of avoiding treachery should be followed on every occasion, even when there is the appearance of an "overbalance of happiness" to be gained by treachery.

This utilitarian argument is plausible. It would therefore not be absurd to agree with Butler that all injustice, treachery, and so on are bad, and should be avoided, whatever promise of good they seem to hold; and that honour, fidelity and justice are always good, even when they seem to be attended by ill consequences; and yet to reject his conclusion that "the whole of virtue" does not consist "in singly aiming ... at promoting the happiness of mankind". For we must distinguish between (1) the rule or rules which should be acted on in particular situations; and (2) the justification of any rule. A utilitarian is not obliged to hold that, in every situation, a man should form an estimate of the happiness and misery which might be produced by different acts, and always act in the light of that estimate so as to maximise happiness and minimise misery. He may hold that actions of certain kinds should always be avoided, and actions of certain other kinds should be

CH. 5 · CONTENT OF MORALITY

performed whenever possible, without any calculation of the particular sequence of happiness and misery which will follow: but that these choices and avoidances are justified by reference to the consequences they tend to have in general. His method of "singly aiming" at promoting happiness would consist of applying rules of conduct whose general good tendency was already established.

Butler — at any rate at the time when he wrote the *Dissertation* — would not have been satisfied with this utilitarian position. His language there makes it clear that he believed certain obligations to exist, whether or not we could satisfy ourselves that we should produce an overbalance of happiness by fulfilling them.

It is tempting to argue that the mysterious witness known as the 'common moral consciousness' sides with Butler. Any proof of the happy or unhappy tendency of a class of actions, taking into account all varieties of circumstances, must be highly speculative. Even if we feel convinced that treachery must, on the whole, produce an overbalance of misery, we cannot exclude the possibility that some unexpected proof to the contrary might be produced. But we feel sure that treachery, cruelty, oppression, and so on, are in themselves morally odious, and that we do not need to wait upon consequences in order to know that they are. Unfortunately we are here in the realm of intuitions. If we are not allowed to appeal to consequences, it is hard to see any ground which could be given, for the moral odiousness of treachery, which would convince a doubter. To Butler, who assumed uniformity of conscience, this point did not seem important. But, surveying mankind at all places and times, we are forced to acknowledge substantial diversity of conscience, and appeals to the common moral consciousness may therefore rest on local idiosyncrasies.

There is a further difficulty in stating this question, arising from the language in which moral qualities are referred to. Butler, though very sensitive to niceties of language, does not seem to have noticed the point — it was perhaps first attended to by Bentham.

§ 2 · LIMITS OF BENEVOLENCE

If we seek to define the names which stand for particular classes of good and bad action, we cannot in the end do so in terms which are morally neutral. Murder is not merely killing, and not merely unprovoked killing; it is wrongful killing. Cruelty is not merely the deliberate infliction of pain: it is infliction of pain for a bad end. Honesty is not merely truthfulness and fulfilment of engagements. Moralists have often proposed cases of conscience in which it seems hard to deny that the truth should be concealed or an engagement broken. An honest man is a man who speaks the truth and pays his debts, except when there is a good reason for doing the contrary. In short, such words as 'cruel', 'treacherous', 'honest', 'loyal', as we commonly understand them, are not mere names for value-bearing qualities. They stand for those actions or characters of a certain class which also have a certain moral value: not for all members of the class indiscriminately.

Thus language insensibly favours those who, like Butler, wish to give a non-utilitarian account of good and bad conduct. For if we ask 'would treachery be wrong, independently of any tendency it may have to lessen happiness?', an affirmative answer is presupposed by our use of the word 'treachery'. This question may be compared with the question 'would poison be dangerous if it did not lead to death?' – though the resemblance is not perfect. If a conspirator repents, and denounces his accomplices, we do not call it treachery. Or, to put the same point in a contrapositive form, if we call it treachery we don't call him a conspirator – we call him, for instance, a member of the resistance movement. Our valuations of conduct are not expressed only in the highly abstract terms to which philosophers have paid most attention – 'good', 'wrong', and so on – but often, perhaps more often, in terms which combine description with moral judgement: 'traitor', 'patriot', 'hero', 'spy', and so on. If we wish to describe conduct and character in morally neutral terms, the resources of ordinary speech often do not enable us to do so except by a good deal of circumlocution.

The difficulty that arises here is not merely the trivial and accidental difficulty of finding or devising a clear and appropriate terminology. It is a deeper difficulty about the analysis of ethical notions. Suppose a number of people join together for a common purpose; and suppose they promise one another, tacitly or expressly, that each of them will fulfil his share of their collective plans, and will do nothing to frustrate them; and suppose one member breaks this undertaking, and discloses the plans of his organisation to some hostile organisation which will use the knowledge to defeat the plans. This general supposition covers a great variety of concrete cases – one general staff over against another; a criminal gang against a police force; a police force against a criminal gang; a business firm against one of its competitors; a political liberation movement against a despotic government; and so on. Does the man who changes sides do wrong? Is he a traitor or a moral hero? We feel these questions can't be answered without a fuller description of the circumstances. But we also feel that the first step, in completing the description, consists of saying whether the people we have imagined were banded together for a good, or at least a harmless purpose, or whether their purpose was nefarious. Here we have passed again from description to valuation. But what is needed now is that those characteristics of their purpose which make it good, innocent, or bad should be described in morally neutral terms. And it seems clear that the descriptions we have given so far are not precise enough. A police force, for instance, does not always pursue good ends; nor are the ends of men banded together against the law always bad. And the virtuousness of a loyal soldier does not seem to depend very closely on the goodness of the cause for which his superiors are fighting.

§ 3 · *Butler's alternative to utilitarianism*

ONE of the attractions of theories of the utilitarian type is that they seem to give us a distinction between good and bad ends in morally neutral terms – in terms, that is, of happiness might hold that a man acts rightly if he acts in a way which does in point of fact tend to produce an overbalance of happiness. An act fulfilling this condition is sometimes described as 'objectively' right. Or we might say that a man acts rightly if he acts in a way which *he expects* to produce an overbalance of happiness. Such actions are sometimes called 'subjectively' right. But neither of these tests seems to be the test which we actually apply, when we consider, in cases of the kinds already mentioned, whether a man who has changed sides has acted treacherously; or whether an act of running away from danger is cowardly. The actual consequences seem irrelevant, except in so far as they throw light on the consequences which the agent might have been expected to foresee. The foreseen consequences we do regard as relevant. But we certainly do not expect a man to fulfil the very stringent requirement of contemplating all the consequences which might be expected to follow, throughout time and space, from each of the actions he might possibly do.

What we require, in the way of expectation of consequences, is that any consequences the agent *did* foresee should be good: or that, if they were bad, he should believe them to be unavoidable. We also require that he shall have exercised 'reasonable foresight'. But that does not mean unlimited foresight. The degree of foresight which we regard as reasonable varies, partly with the capacities of the agent, and partly with the importance of the field within which he is acting. We expect both fuller and more accurate foresight of intelligent and well-informed people, and more limited foresight of others. And we expect the consequences to be weighed more carefully when a man is, for example, taking a step which might affect someone else's life or health, than when he is playing a game.

Here Butler is much closer, for what it is worth, to the 'common moral consciousness' than the utilitarians are. For Butler, as we have seen, trusts the conscientious choice of a "plain honest man". And we can be pretty sure that very few plain honest men ever enter into the elaborate balancing of remote consequences which a utilitarian would prescribe.

§ 3 · ALTERNATIVE TO UTILITARIANISM

and unhappiness. A change of sides, to continue the same example, is bad, and is treachery, if it tends to lessen human happiness, or if the man who changes sides supposes that it does; and in the contrary case it is not treachery, and is morally good or at least innocent.

Butler would reply that the moral odiousness of treachery can be discerned independently of any elaborate calculation of consequences. He did not raise the important question of the meaning of such words as 'treachery', and the criterion by which we are to distinguish those cases of changing sides which are morally odious from those which are not. Had he done so, he might perhaps have argued on these lines. When we reflect, we can recognise certain graces of character and conduct, and certain deformities, which have a moral value of their own. These qualities manifest themselves in right or wrong appreciation of the various situations in which a man may be placed. 'Loyalty' is the name of a certain grace of character, and 'treachery' of a certain deformity of character: different from other graces and deformities of character, whose names are, for instance, 'generosity' and 'meanness', or 'courage' and 'cowardice'. We cannot give any general formula describing the manner in which one of these qualities will be manifested in all possible situations. But we can give examples, by the help of which the meanings of the names can be recognised. Treachery very often involves a change of sides, and loyalty a refusal to change sides: courage often involves facing danger, and cowardice avoiding it. But there are some situations in which a loyal man will change sides, or a brave man run away from danger, without his loyalty or courage being impaired. When a man fails to recognise the differences in conduct suitable to diverse situations, we do not call him brave or loyal without qualification; we speak of 'blind' or 'irrational' or 'perverse' courage or loyalty.

The utilitarian analysis does not combine easily with our common ways of regarding these qualities of character. For according to utilitarians, there are only two possible distinctions between virtuous and vicious conduct and character. We

§ 3 · ALTERNATIVE TO UTILITARIANISM

There is even, in Butler's view, a moral danger in probing over curiously into the rights and wrongs of alternative actions. "That which is called considering what is our duty in a particular case is very often nothing but endeavouring to explain it away. Thus those courses which, if men would fairly attend to the dictates of their own consciences, they would see to be corruption, excess, oppression, uncharitableness; these are refined upon – things were so and so circumstantiated – great difficulties are raised about fixing bounds and degrees: and thus every moral obligation whatever may be evaded. Here is scope, I say, for an unfair mind to explain away every moral obligation to itself" (*S*. 7.14). This passage is not directed expressly against utilitarian views. But it is plainly applicable to them in the form they more commonly take. We have suggested that a utilitarian might hold that the good or bad tendency of certain classes of action can be taken as already established on general grounds, and that these generalisations can be summed up in rules, which may be acted on without nice calculation of consequences on every occasion. Those who acted on such rules would not be in danger of explaining away their obligations in the way Butler describes. But this seems a feeble kind of utilitarianism. It would be plausible to hold that there is a large class of actions about which we can safely assume that they seldom have momentous consequences of any kind – washing one's hands, drinking a cup of tea, going for a walk, buying a newspaper – the thousand and one trivialities of daily life which usually we hardly contemplate as distinct subjects of choice. But it is not in such matters that searching of conscience, and the danger of explaining away duty, are likely to arise. If we consider some of the modes of action which most moralists have agreed in considering momentous – speaking the truth, causing pain, using or failing to use one's talents, keeping promises, injuring a man's reputation, supporting one's dependents, and so on – it seems much harder to suppose that we can always deal with these matters so as to produce an "overbalance of happiness" simply by applying an established rule, without estimation of

CH. 5 · CONTENT OF MORALITY

particular consequences. But if, on all momentous occasions, we are to make a thoroughgoing utilitarian calculation of consequences, the danger Butler speaks of will exist.

Butler is, of course, presupposing that a plain honest man *can* usually know how he should act without elaborate calculation. On a utilitarian view he cannot. A utilitarian is therefore forced to say, either that the danger of explaining away duty, as described by Butler, does not exist, or that, if it does, it is unavoidable: elaborate calculation is the only way of knowing how one should act; and if men who make the necessary calculations are apt to be misled by self-partiality there is nevertheless no other method they can use. But we may well think that the danger Butler points to is grave and undeniable, that a method attended by this danger cannot be the only possible method of settling questions of conscience, and that its existence is a reason against thoroughgoing utilitarianism.

CHAPTER 6

DESERT

§ 1 · *Butler's assumptions*

IT cannot be said that Butler has a theory of desert. He uses the notion, but on the whole uses it uncritically. He assumes that there is a direct moral relation between wrongdoing and liability to punishment. That a wrongdoer should be punished is just, not because he has been warned, by human or Divine law, that a certain penalty will follow a certain deed, but simply because he has knowingly done wrong. "It is not foreknowledge of the punishment which renders us obnoxious to it; but merely violating a known obligation" (*Pr.* 29). Something of the same sort seems to be implied in the famous passage on the authority of conscience (*S.* 2.8), where he writes that conscience, when it "approves or condemns", "goes on to anticipate a higher and more effectual sentence, which shall hereafter second and affirm its own". A man who knows he has done wrong knows also, Butler seems to mean, that he deserves punishment. The same doctrine is clearly stated in the *Dissertation* and the *Analogy*. "Upon considering or viewing together our notion of vice and that of misery, there results a third, that of ill-desert" (*D. on V.* 3). In this passage, he insists that, when we speak of a man as deserving punishment, what we mean is not that his punishment serves some good purpose. "For if unhappily it were resolved that a man who, by some innocent action, was infected with the plague should be left to perish, lest by other people's coming near him the infection should spread, no one would say he deserved this treatment."

In the *Analogy*, he assumes that the existence of a relation of desert depends upon the freedom of the will. If someone

[127]

were brought up to believe in "necessity", he would "conclude that since he cannot possibly behave otherwise than he does he is not a subject of blame or commendation, nor can deserve to be rewarded or punished" (*An.* 1.6.6). If "the opinion of necessity" were true, punishment would not be deserved; but neither would it be unjust. For no acts would be just or unjust, neither those of the culprit nor those of his judges (*An.* 1.6.8).

§ 2 · *The meaning of "freedom" and "necessity"*

UNFORTUNATELY Butler gives no positive account of the meaning of "freedom" and "necessity". He does not seem to have noticed that, as most modern writers would agree, there is a good deal of ambiguity in the use of these words. He seems to have assumed that to believe in necessity is equivalent to believing in what later writers would call universal causation, or determinism, or the reign of law: and that if that principle were true there could be no such thing as freedom or desert. Although the proper analysis of freedom is still in dispute, there would probably be fairly wide agreement on the following points.

1. If someone deserves certain treatment because of a certain action, it follows that in *some* sense he acted freely.

2. Similarly, it follows that in *some* sense his action was not necessary, or he was under no necessity of acting in the way he did.

3. But it is not certain that it follows, either from proposition (1) or from proposition (2), that his action was not causally determined.

4. And it is not certain that, if an action *were* not causally determined, a person could properly be said to *deserve* any particular treatment on account of that action.

Each of these statements needs to be amplified. (1) It is fairly easy to think of cases in which we shall deny that someone acted freely, and take this denial as a reason for denying

§ 2 · "FREEDOM" AND "NECESSITY"

that he deserves praise or blame. If I slip on a piece of orange peel, and in slipping knock down a bystander, it will be agreed that I didn't act freely and don't deserve blame. And if denial of freedom implies denial of desert, then, as proposition (1) states, assertion of desert must imply assertion of freedom. But it is much harder to give examples in which the assertion of freedom is unquestionably justified. For as soon as we rise above the level of unfreedom of the man who slips on a piece of orange peel – the level, that is, of purely mechanical forces acting on his body – we seem obliged to recognise that the question whether a man was free does not depend solely on the question how his action was caused. A man often makes the excuse 'I was not free to act otherwise' although he has been under no physical constraint. Sometimes what has limited his freedom is an obligation – a promise, for example, or the law of the land, or a moral precept. Sometimes it is a threat, or the equivalent of a threat. For example, a man might justify a failure to keep an appointment on the ground that he had stopped to help someone injured in a street accident, or that he had been summoned to appear before a law court. Here what is supposed to have limited his freedom is an alleged obligation. Or he might explain that to keep the appointment he would have had to leave his factory at a certain hour, and that his employer had threatened him with dismissal unless he stayed to work overtime. We sometimes regard one or the other of these kinds of excuse as quite satisfactory, and then we say 'yes, I recognise that you weren't free'. On the other hand, we may say 'I don't agree, I think you *were* quite free to keep your appointment'. In either case, our acceptance or rejection of the excuse implies a moral judgement. It is not purely – perhaps not at all – a statement as to the manner in which the action in question was caused. We are judging either that the unfulfilled obligation could rightly be overridden, or that it could not, by some competing obligation, or by the burdensomeness of fulfilling it. We may wish to say, for instance, 'your obligation to meet me as you promised was stronger than your obligation to attend to the man you saw knocked over': or we may wish to say 'I agree that you weren't obliged to keep your promise to me at the expense of losing your job'.

It is clear that what is at issue here is not the psychological mechanism by which the choice was produced. If one party claims, in such cases as we have supposed, '*A was* free to act otherwise', and the other '*A* was *not* free', there is no reason why they should disagree about the causation of *A*'s action. This is why it is hard to find undoubted specimens of a choice which a man was free to make differently, in the sense of 'free' which has now become manifest. The reason is that no amount of precise specification of the agent's history, circumstances, and state of mind, will settle the question. The moral allowability of his choice remains open to dispute, and it is upon the settlement of *that* question that his freedom or unfreedom to act otherwise depends.

If this were the only sense of the word 'free' involved in proposition (1), the substance of that proposition would be that a man only deserves unfavourable treatment if he has done wrong; and presumably, *pari ratione*, that he only deserves favourable treatment if he has done right. A similar interpretation can be given for proposition (2). When it is said that a man was under no necessity to act in a certain way, it may be implied that he was under no obligation to act in that way; or that to act in a contrary way would not have been unduly burdensome. If he makes the counter claim 'it was necessary for me to act as I did', he implies, either that to act in a contrary way would have been excessively disadvantageous to him, or that he was under an obligation to act as he did.

If no more than this is involved in propositions (1) and (2), it follows that there is no special connection between the notion of desert and the notions of freedom and necessity interpreted in some causal sense. The connection, if any, will hold between freedom and necessity in the moral sense we have pointed out, on the one hand, and on the other hand a complex of other moral notions, including desert, obligation,

§ 2 · "FREEDOM" AND "NECESSITY"

duty, responsibility, and so on. This may well be the case. But by a further analysis of the connection between the ideas of freedom and necessity and that of desert we can illustrate sufficiently clearly their connection with moral notions in general. We shall incidentally throw light on propositions (3) and (4).

When we think about human conduct, not as moralists, but as biologists or psychologists or sociologists, we usually assume that every feature of all human conduct is causally determined; that is, we apply in this particular sphere the general assumption known as universal causation, determinism, or the reign of law. Although this assumption is not hard to understand, or to apply in practice, it is hard to state precisely, and we must be content here with a rather vague formulation of it. The statement that a certain event is completely determined is equivalent to a statement which will be set out shortly. Let us write 'E' for the event in question, and '$C_1, C_2, \ldots$', etc., for any conditions connected with the occurrence of E. Then there is a law – that is a universally true proposition – from which it may be deduced that if certain conditions, C_1, C_2, etc., are fulfilled, an event just like E occurs. It follows that if E had been different in any respects, at least one of the conditions, C_1, C_2, etc., would not have been fulfilled. The reason for this rather cumbersome formulation is that the law in question cannot properly be expressed by reference to E alone, or to events just like E. Every event possesses a number of variable qualities in just one determinate form. The law, in any advanced science, will be so formulated that, from given values of certain variables, determinate values of other variables can be deduced. The qualities of a particular event are only one out of infinitely many possible sets of qualities which would be specifications of the variables in the same law. It is conceivable that an event should be determined in many respects, but not completely determined. In that case, while some of its qualities would be deducible from the relevant law, one at least would not.

CH. 6 · DESERT

An event, then, is said to be completely determined if it is related to a universal law in the way which has just been indicated. Determinism is the doctrine that every event which has occurred, is occurring, or will occur, was, is or will be completely determined. Indeterminism is the doctrine that at least one event was, is, or will be not completely determined. Of course, indeterminists usually hold that, not just one event, but a very large number, are not completely determined. (A more precise analysis of determinism may be found in *Determinism, indeterminism and libertarianism*, by C. D. Broad.)

In the rest of this discussion, it will be convenient to speak of an event as 'determined' rather than as 'caused'. The reason is that, among the conditions to which an event is related by some law, only a limited selection are commonly spoken of as 'causes'; and the selection is made in the light of our practical interests. There is no precise rule for picking out the causes among all the relevant conditions. An example will make this clear. Suppose we want to know the causes of a road accident. Someone interested chiefly in human conduct, a policeman for instance, may say quite truly that it was caused by the carelessness of a motorist. But a motor engineer may say, with equal truth, that the accident was caused by faulty brakes, and a road engineer that it was caused by a wet road surface. Making the usual deterministic assumptions, we can easily recognise that each of these statements, though not false, is incomplete; and that even the more sophisticated statement, that the carelessness, the brakes, and the road surface were all contributing causes, is still very incomplete. The exact form of the event depended on all the working parts of the car, the wind, the atmosphere, the light, and perhaps many other conditions of which we know nothing. When we speak of *the* cause we usually have in mind some feature of the situation which is humanly controllable, and such that, if it had been substantially different, the event would have been substantially different.

§ 3 · *Determinism and indeterminism*

It is, then, very commonly assumed, outside ethical discussions, that all features of all human conduct are completely determined. It follows that, though human choices and acts of will may be among the determining conditions of many human actions, these choices must themselves have been determined. If we go far enough back in time, we must reach a point at which they were determined wholly by conditions which did not include choices on the part of the person concerned – unless we are prepared to suppose an infinite sequence of choices on his part, stretching back before his birth. And though this last supposition may not be indefensible, it is seldom defended.

Although, in a scientific mood, many people would be content to accept this consequence of determinism, in a moralising mood they often feel dissatisfied with it. For it seems to follow that, in a very important sense, no one could ever act otherwise than in fact he does act. It may be true, of any voluntary act, that if the agent had decided otherwise he would have acted otherwise: and it may be true that, if on some earlier occasion he had chosen or acted otherwise – so that his character was to that extent modified – he would on this occasion have decided otherwise. We can properly suppose that his present act is determined in part by his present choice, and his present choice by earlier choices, themselves determined in the same way throughout a long sequence. But ultimately – that is, if we go far enough back – we have to conclude that the whole sequence of decisions and actions was wholly determined by conditions in which his will and character had no share. And so, whenever we say that a man might have acted differently, we are only entitled to imply that he would have done so *if* some state of affairs outside himself had been different. From this it is commonly thought to follow that, in the sense referred to in propositions (1) and (2), men never act freely but always necessarily, and consequently that

[133]

no one ever deserves this or that treatment because of his actions. If Butler's phrase "the opinion of necessity" (*An.* 1.6) means, or at least includes, determinism – as I think it does – then Butler assumed that these consequences follow. Many people think it so obvious that men have deserts that they take this train of reasoning as a disproof of determinism. We have seen already that, according to Butler, a child reared in necessitarian principles would deduce that he never deserved blame or punishment. Perhaps the old saying '*tout comprendre, c'est tout pardonner*' sums up the supposed force of the foregoing reasoning.

If this reasoning is sound, it leads to destructive conclusions, not only about desert, but also about a catena of other moral notions. If we conclude that no one ever acts freely, we may readily pass to the further conclusions that no actions are right or wrong – for the statement that I acted rightly implies that I might have acted wrongly, and *vice versa*; that there are no obligations – for I am only obliged to do what I *can* do, and there would be no sense in talking of obligations unless they are capable of being either fulfilled or unfulfilled; and that no one is ever responsible for his actions.

Yet the alternative to the premisses on which the foregoing reasoning rested seems no better. It is the assertion of indeterminism, in the particular form of the assertion that some actions or some decisions are partly undetermined. That would imply that, even if a man's character and decision and circumstances had been exactly what in fact they were, a different action might have followed; or that, even if his character and circumstances and previous history had been exactly what in fact they were, a different decision might have occurred. In that case, it would follow that a man whose actions were criticised might justly reply 'but my actions don't depend on my decisions; for however I decide, one action may ensue or another may ensue': or 'my decisions don't depend on my character; for whatever my character may be, one or another of several decisions might occur'. This seems no more consistent with the common notions of desert and responsibility than the determinist position.

§ 3 · DETERMINISM AND INDETERMINISM

The same point is expressed, perhaps a little less precisely, but more eloquently, by Hume (*Treatise of human nature*, 2.3.2). "The constant and universal object of hatred or anger is a person or creature endowed with thought and consciousness; and when any criminal or injurious actions excite that passion, 'tis only by their relation to the person or connection with him. But according to the doctrine of liberty or chance this connection is reduced to nothing, nor are men more accountable for those actions which are designed and premeditated than for such as are the most casual and accidental. Actions are by their very nature temporary and perishing; and where they proceed not from some cause in the characters and disposition of the person who performed them they infix not themselves upon him, and can neither redound to his honour, if good, nor infamy, if evil. The action itself may be blameable; it may be contrary to all the rules of morality and religion: but the person is not responsible for it; and as it proceeded from nothing in him that is durable or constant, and leaves nothing of that nature behind it, 'tis impossible he can, upon its account, become the object of punishment or vengeance. According to the hypothesis of liberty, therefore, a man is as pure and untainted, after having committed the most horrid crimes, as at the first moment of his birth, nor is his character any way concerned in his actions; since they are not derived from it, and the wickedness of the one can never be used as a proof of the depravity of the other. 'Tis only upon the principles of necessity that a person acquires any merit or demerit from his actions, however the common opinion may incline to the contrary."

It is hard to see the way out of this deadlock. If we wish to hold, as Butler probably did, that when we speak of desert we refer to an unanalysable moral relation between an agent, or his acts, and a consequence of some kind, we are at least no worse off if we accept the deterministic alternative than if we accept indeterminism. We shall have to hold that the existence of this relation is discerned by a special kind of moral insight. If we treat common ideas of desert as embodying this insight, we shall, indeed, be in difficulties about accepting determinism: but they are no greater than those presented by the combination of common ideas of desert with indeterminism.

§ 4 · *The utilitarian theory of desert*

A WAY out may be sought by attempting an analysis of desert.

It would be agreed by all moral philosophers that an action cannot be morally judgeable unless it depends in some way on the agent's will. It need not be the direct outcome of a decision, for it would be agreed that negligences as well as positive acts are morally judgeable. But if a piece of negligence is to be morally judgeable, it must be of a kind which would have been avoided, if a certain decision had been made. This relation to the will of an agent is part of the meaning of the word 'moral'.

We have seen that, when the question is raised whether someone was or was not free to act in a certain way, the answer depends on a balancing of one or more obligations, and of the impediments to fulfilling them. If A says 'I was not free to do X', and B says 'you were', they are not disputing as to the dependence of the action on A's will, for that is presupposed by both parties. In the limiting case in which A is physically prevented from doing X, the dispute will not arise. When A claims that he was not free to keep an engagement, on the ground that he was morally debarred from keeping it by some stronger obligation, or that he was not morally required to keep it at an excessive cost to himself, he assumes in either case that, if he had chosen to do what he was morally debarred from doing, or not morally obliged to do, he would have done it.

When B, who condemns A's action, claims that he was free to act otherwise, he may go on to say that A is responsible for the wrong he has done, and that he deserves to suffer certain consequences. These further steps in B's condemnation of A open possibilities of a good many counter pleas on A's part,

§ 4 · UTILITARIAN THEORY OF DESERT

which need not be surveyed in detail. Without doing so, we can see that *B* is adding to the moral judgement which he expressed when he said that *A* was free to refrain from the condemned action. He is adding that, since *A* has done what he ought not to have done, other people ought, or are morally entitled, to act towards him in a certain way – perhaps by blaming him, or penalising him – for instance by avoiding his company, or not relying on his word in future, or by demanding some sort of compensation from him.

Without raising any speculative questions about the causation of conduct, it is possible to justify these additional moral judgements on utilitarian lines. It may be taken as established that blame and penalties – as also praise and rewards – tend to influence the will; and that the attaching of these sanctions to right and wrong actions will tend to strengthen habits of acting rightly and weaken habits of acting wrongly. (Whether blaming and penalising are the best method of achieving these ends in a given case, or in most cases, is another question, to which the answer is much less certain.) And it might be argued that, when we say a man is responsible, and has certain deserts, the whole meaning of our statement can be resolved into two clauses: (1) he has done a good or bad action, or a right or wrong action; (2) it is useful to apply certain sanctions to him – useful, that is, in the way of influencing his habits and other people's. Men are responsible only for voluntary acts, and for voluntarily avoidable negligences, because those are the only features of their conduct which can be influenced by sanctions. This is a psychological fact, which only came to be discerned comparatively late in the development of men's ethical thinking: we know of primitive societies in which sanctions are annexed to the consequences of men's conduct, whether they were voluntarily avoidable or not.

But the notion of a voluntarily avoidable negligence is perhaps not so simple as it might appear at first glance. We think it obvious that if I send a man a letter, and he opens it by candlelight, and when he does so the letter catches fire, his clothes catch fire from the letter, and he is burnt to death,

[137]

I am in no degree at all responsible for his death. And if I drop a piece of orange peel in the street, and someone slips on it and is killed, though it may be thought that I ought to have been more careful, I am still far from being held gravely responsible. But if I thoughtlessly drive a car at high speed past a red traffic signal, and kill a man crossing the road, I may be convicted of manslaughter. Obviously, in each of these cases it might be said that I could have prevented the consequences of my act, for if I had decided against sending the letter I should not have sent it, and if I had reminded myself not to drop orange peel I should have put it in some safe receptacle: so in each case what happened was voluntarily avoidable. But we do not call each of these a case of *negligence*: the third is undoubtedly such a case, the first undoubtedly is not, and the second is dubious. What we mean by 'negligence' is of the same order as what we mean by 'was free to do otherwise'. The statement that a man was negligent in a certain matter is not a description of the psychological mechanism of his action: it expresses a moral judgement. The question whether an action was done in a state of euphoria and general inattentiveness, or in a methodical and calculating frame of mind, is not as such relevant to the question whether a man acted negligently. He acted negligently if he was generally inattentive when he ought to have been attending to some particular matter; but so he did if he was methodical and attentive, but didn't attend to an object he ought to have attended to. When we make a judgement of negligence, we apply a moral principle of a certain general class which might be called 'rules of circumspection'. Most of us assume that the only rules of circumspection about letter-writing relate to style and content, and not to the physical effects of handling a letter. But it is not impossible to conceive circumstances in which we should think otherwise. Suppose, for example, it were found that the handling of certain rare types of paper produced a skin disease in a certain rare type of person, we should readily come to think that some circumspection about the physical effects was obligatory. On the other hand, most

§ 4 · UTILITARIAN THEORY OF DESERT

of us assume already that a very high degree of circumspection about the physical effects of driving a car is obligatory.

Thus, a piece of negligence or circumspection constitutes a bad or good action if there is an obligation to be circumspect in the relevant circumstances. Habits of circumspection, or the lack of them, are modifiable by people's acts of will, and people may therefore be responsible for negligence in the same way as they are responsible for actions in the more obvious sense.

There is one further point which may well be added to the utilitarian analysis of desert and responsibility. Although, on this view, the two clauses already set out convey the whole of our meaning when we ascribe responsibility or desert, they are not the whole of what we have in mind. We tend to feel repugnance towards bad actions and those who do them, and to have friendly and warm feelings towards those who do good actions. We wish the former ill and we wish the latter well. If wrongdoers prosper we feel defrauded or even outraged, and so we do if good men suffer. Thus, as long as it remains true that it is useful to penalise a wrongdoer and to reward or praise a good man, our spontaneous feelings back up the policy which, on utilitarian grounds, ought to be adopted. But suppose, in exceptional cases, it were established that penalties for the bad and rewards for the virtuous would do more harm than good, our sentiments would not be correspondingly reapportioned: we should still wish the good to prosper and the bad to suffer. In consequence, we come to feel that there is a sort of intrinsic tie between the moral value of a man's character or conduct and the way in which he ought to be treated.

It would, as Butler points out, seem absurd to say that a man who has not done wrong *deserves* ill treatment (*D. on V. 3*, quoted above). There are two reasons for this, according to the theory we have outlined. (1) Our theory asserts that a statement about desert contains two elements. It is not simply a statement that to treat a man in a specified way will be useful. It includes also a statement that he has acted well or badly.

CH. 6 · DESERT

We do not use such words as 'deserve' unless we are implying both that a man's conduct is bad and that to penalise him is useful, or both that his conduct is good and to praise or reward him is useful. (2) If, as Butler says, "it were unhappily resolved that a man ... infected with the plague should be left to perish", our emotional attitude to that decision would be very different from our attitude to the punishing of wrongdoers: and the word 'deserve' would seem inappropriate from its association with, and its function as an expression of, the latter emotional attitude.

It is clear that Butler would not accept this analysis of desert, in terms of the usefulness of sanctions and our emotional attitudes to people's conduct. He would regard it as an explaining away of desert. Punishment, quite apart from its usefulness, is intrinsically required by wrongdoing. Desert is a two-termed relation, between a wrongdoer of a certain description and a penalty of a certain description. But according to the utilitarian view it is a three-termed relation, between a wrongdoer, a penalty, and the consequences of the penalty. Or we may put the same point, if we like, by saying that, in Butler's view, deserving is a three-termed relation between a person, his wrong act, and a penalty – A, the agent, deserves P, the penalty, because of W, the wrong act: but on this analysis the utilitarian theory will make deserving a four-termed relation – A deserves P because C, the consequence of P, tends to discourage such acts as W.

The attraction of the utilitarian theory is that it lays all questions about particular deserts open to rational discussion, and that it does not require any obscure assumption about the causation of actions. A man deserves blame or penalties only in respect of actions he was free to avoid. On the utilitarian view, this principle does not refer to any special causal mechanism, or absence of causal mechanism: it implies only that the action was not one he was obliged to do, and not one which it would have been excessively costly to him not to do. It is only required that he should have been free in the moral sense of the word 'free' which we have pointed out.

[140]

§ 4 · UTILITARIAN THEORY OF DESERT

Butler's view of desert, if developed, must make large claims for intuition. That a certain wrongdoer deserves a certain punishment is not an assertion for or against which grounds can be given – by considering, for example, the probable effects of different types of punishment. It is an assertion whose truth has to be discerned by the same "sentiment of the understanding or perception of the heart" by which the wrongness of the act was discerned. And if the relation of desert only held between a wrongdoer and some unspecified penalty – light or severe, short or prolonged – desert would be a trivial notion. If desert is not to be trivial, there must be a power of discerning, not merely that a wrongdoer deserves punishment, but that a wrongdoer of a certain description, or a certain degree of guilt, deserves a penalty of a specifiable kind and amount.

We must also depend on intuition as our only means of discovering the relation between desert and causation. Butler, and many other moralists, hold that if men have deserts their actions cannot be completely determined: desert is incompatible with universal causation. But since no analysis of desert can be given, we cannot see how this incompatibility arises. It must itself, like the relation of desert, be directly discerned.

Because Butler's views about desert and freedom imply that a large range of moral truths can only be known intuitively, it does not follow that he is mistaken. But we are entitled to wish to reduce the intuitive element in ethics: for whatever is brought within the realm of intuition is taken out of the realm of argument. Once an intuitionistic view is accepted, about a particular class of judgements, the only form of discussion which remains possible is the comparing of notes about people's intuitions.

CHAPTER 7

THE PLACE OF GOD IN BUTLER'S ETHICS

§ 1 · *Butler's characteristic ethical teaching non-theological*

As we have illustrated in the preceding chapters, it is possible to extract from Butler's writings a moral philosophy conceived in purely natural terms: that is to say, in which there is, or need be, no mention of the supernatural. This is what his own statement of his method implies (*Pr.* 12): that method starts "from a matter of fact, namely what the particular nature of man is ...; from whence it proceeds to determine what course of life it is which is correspondent to this whole nature".

Butler did not hold that ethical notions can be analysed in terms of God's will. The words 'good' and 'right' do not mean 'what God desires or commands'; and 'bad' and 'wrong' do not mean 'what displeases God or is forbidden by God'. That God wills what is good and right is a synthetic statement, not a tautology. And the goodness or rightness of an action is a self-sufficient reason for doing it: our reason for doing what is right and avoiding what is wrong does not arise from providential rewards and penalties. There are well known logical difficulties in any theory which defines goodness or duty in terms of a divine fiat. If the name 'good' or 'right' merely stands for what God wills, every statement about the goodness or righteousness of God reduces itself to the tautology that God wills what he wills. It then follows that if we call God good we do not imply that he is of any particular character – for example loving, benevolent, just, merciful – rather than of any other – for example, cruel, malicious, oppressive, deceitful. Whatever God's moral

§ 1 · BUTLER'S ETHICS NON-THEOLOGICAL

character might be, it would remain true that he was good. And there are well known ethical objections to any theory which makes the bindingness of duty depend on rewards and penalties, so that duty or moral goodness is entirely resolved into prudence. Butler did, indeed, hold that in the long run a dutiful and a prudent course of action entirely coincided: but our obligation to act as we ought is not to be identified with the fact that it is prudent so to act.

This, on the whole, is Butler's teaching, so that on the whole he escapes the objections which have been pointed out. But there are one or two passages which seem to have a contrary tendency. They belong to Butler's discussions of the limitations of benevolence as a universal rule of conduct (see chapter 5, § 2). For example, in *S.* 12.31 fn. he writes "though the good of the creation be the only end of the Author of it, yet *He may have laid us under particular obligations* which we may discern and feel ourselves under, quite distinct from a perception that the observance or violation of them is for the happiness or misery of our fellow-creatures" (my italics). The point is elaborated in *D. on V.* 8–10, where Butler argues that the fact that we approve and disapprove of actions independently of their tendency to promote happiness shows that God designed that we should do so: and this design is taken as proof that we are obliged to act according to those approvals and disapprovals.

These passages might lead us to infer that the statement 'we are under an obligation to do so and so' means that God intends or commands us to do so and so. If that interpretation were accepted, serious difficulties would arise. Butler would either have to abandon the principle of "the moral fitness and unfitness of actions, prior to all will whatever; which I apprehend ... to determine the Divine conduct" (*An.* 2.8.11); or he would have to maintain that terms of moral valuation – 'fitness', 'duty', and so on – have totally distinct meanings according as they are applied to God or to human beings.

But it seems possible to interpret these passages more consistently with Butler's general teaching. The expression 'to

[143]

CH. 7 · GOD IN BUTLER'S ETHICS

lay someone under an obligation' need not be used with God as its subject. I may lay someone under an obligation by doing him a service: he is then said to owe me a debt of gratitude. Again, a person entitled to give orders can lay an obligation upon those to whom he gives them. A judge who allows bail to an accused person lays an obligation upon him to appear in court on a specified day. In such cases as these we cannot properly say that an obligation is created. When *A* gives an order to *B*, the obligation under which *B* lies is not reducible to the fact that *A* has given an order. *A* can only lay an obligation on *B* in virtue of some pre-existing obligation – for example, an obligation upon all men to obey lawfully appointed judges; or to show gratitude to their benefactors. The act of *A* which lays an obligation upon *B* brings this pre-existing obligation into play: it creates, not the obligation, but a situation of the type to which the obligation applies.

It seems possible to place a similar interpretation on Butler's statements about the obligations under which God lays us. The reason why we lie under them is not that it is God's will that we should act in this or that way and to be obliged is by definition to be willed by God to act in a certain way; but that he has made us beings of a certain nature, and to beings of that nature a certain conduct is morally fitting, this fittingness being "prior to all will whatever".

On this interpretation, the non-supernatural character of Butler's ethics is unimpaired. He does not require that we shall know God's will, by revelation or in some other manner, in order to deduce our duty from it. Moral insight is an independent source of knowledge. Nor does he require that in order to have a reason for doing what, on reflection, we know we ought to do we shall be assured that to do our duty will providentially be made worth our while. The knowledge that we ought to act in a certain way is in itself a sufficient reason for so acting.

But although Butler's ethical teaching can stand on its own feet, it is moulded by belief in God in certain ways. In the

§ 1 · BUTLER'S ETHICS NON-THEOLOGICAL

first place, that belief assures us that the world is morally ordered. We know on independent grounds, that virtue should be rewarded and vice punished (see chapter 6). If that does not take place, in the long run, justice is not done. Our moral insight can tell us what a just administration of the world would be, but not that the world is justly administered. From observation of men and things, we see that there is some tendency for the good to prosper and the wicked to come to harm – there is a certain *poena naturalis* observable in the course of nature – but we cannot discern that, without exception, men's destinies are proportioned to their deserts. But if there is a God, and if he is the providential ruler of the world, we can be assured that "all shall be set right at the final distribution of things" (*S.* 3.8). The universe is justly administered, and in the end what we see to be just will be fully and perfectly realised.

§ 2 · *Final causes*

A SECOND theological feature of Butler's ethics is the appeal he sometimes makes to final causes. He occasionally departs from his normal method, the scrutiny of human nature, and draws ethical conclusions from the supposed purposes of particular elements in the human constitution. These finalistic passages are on the whole the weakest in the *Sermons*. For example, in *Sermon 6*, on compassion, Butler argues that by attending to human nature and the circumstances of human life we can discover the final cause of an "affection" – that is, we can discover for what end God constituted men so as to possess that affection. From this knowledge of the final cause, we can deduce "what course of life we are made for, what is our duty" (*S.* 6.1). The final cause of compassion is "to prevent and to relieve misery" (*S.* 6.3). That is, God framed men as compassionate beings in order that there should be some relief from the miseries to which their circumstances expose them. Knowing that that was God's intention, we can infer

CH. 7 · GOD IN BUTLER'S ETHICS

that this exercise of compassion is a duty. Compassion would be diverted from its right end if it led us to close our minds to people's sufferings, for the sake of avoiding sympathetic distress.

This line of argument is not characteristic and puts our knowledge of our duties on much shakier ground than that on which it rests in Butler's more characteristic passages. For how are we to know what is the final cause of any feature of the world, for example, a human passion? There seem to be only two possible methods. We may note all the effects it actually has; or we may note the good effects it is capable of having. But by the first method no contribution could be made to our moral knowledge. For if the final cause of a passion is to produce all the effects it actually does produce, no distinction can be drawn between fulfilment of purpose and non-fulfilment. And so no further conclusion can be reached, that one type of conduct is good, and another type bad, because one fulfils and the other fails to fulfil a divine purpose. For all conduct will equally fulfil it. The second method cannot be applied except by including moral judgements among our premisses. We need to know in advance that some effects are good, and others are bad, and we may then go on to infer that the final cause, the divinely ordained purpose, of a passion is to produce the good effects only. But we cannot use this conclusion as an independent means of distinguishing the use of a passion from its abuse, for we have already supposed ourselves qualified to draw that distinction in order to reach our conclusion about the final cause.

Even if we had some means of knowing final causes independently of the two methods just outlined, there would be a further difficulty. Suppose we know God's purpose to be of a certain nature: suppose, for example, we know that he intends us to indulge our feelings of compassion in such a manner as to lessen human misery. That knowledge would only support the conclusion that we *ought* to relieve misery on one or another of three assumptions. (1) It might be held that 'duty' or 'what we ought to do' means, by definition, whatever God

§ 2 · FINAL CAUSES

wishes or commands. It would follow that the statement that we ought to act in this or that way, because God commands it, would be tautologous: it would be equivalent to the statement 'since this is commanded, this is commanded'. We have already seen that this opinion was rejected by Butler (*e.g. An.* 2.8.11). (2) It might be held that 'duty' means, by definition, whatever will pay us best in the long run. If we know that we shall be rewarded or punished according as we have obeyed or failed to obey God's commands, it follows that to obey those commands is our duty. But Butler's rejection of this definition of duty is clear, both from the whole tenor of his discussion of the authority of conscience, and from many passages in the *Analogy* (*e.g. An.* 1.7.11). (3) It might be held that, though duty is definable neither in terms of God's commands nor in terms of our interests, we know that God is perfectly good, and whatever he commands is right. In that case, we might theoretically have two distinct methods of knowing our duty: by the exercise of conscience, and by deduction from God's commands. The results of these two methods might always coincide, or they might sometimes conflict, or there might be instances in which one method was fruitful and the other was not. In the first case one method or the other would be superfluous. And since the exercise of conscience is supposed to be open to everyone, whether or not he has independent means of knowing God's commands, that method would be the more generally useful. In the second case, there would be a conflict of authority such as Butler never contemplates, and assumes to be impossible. Conscience is "the guide assigned us by the Author of our nature" (*S.* 3.5). It is only in the third case that knowledge of God's commands, deduced from knowledge of final causes, might be independently useful to us as a means of knowing our duty. Butler does not distinctly contemplate this possibility, and it would hardly be compatible with his general teaching: since all that he says, in the most fully developed passages of the *Sermons* and the *Dissertation*, suggests not only the reliability but the sufficiency of conscience.

CH. 7 · GOD IN BUTLER'S ETHICS

I conclude that, except on assumptions very foreign to Butler's, any attempt to deduce duties from final causes is misconceived.

§ 3 · *The goodness of human nature*

BUTLER's discussions of final causes rest on an assumption whose grounds would perhaps be dogmatic rather than empirical. It is that there are no tendencies – no "principles" or "passions" – in human nature which are inherently bad. There are no tendencies, therefore, which it is our duty simply to stifle. And Butler does not think of the passions as, so to speak, a neutral raw material from which a good or a bad character may be fashioned. Every passion has a *prima facie* claim to be exercised. For every passion there are possibilities of good exercise and of abuse. We survey these possibilities when we consider how to make ourselves "most easy to ourselves", and when we consider "what becomes such creatures as we are": and the results, whether reached by self-love or by conscience, are substantially the same. A particular exercise of any passion may have to be repressed or modified, whether because it frustrates too many of my other passions or because it is injurious to my fellow men. But the ultimate objective of any passion is good, though it may be sought by the help of evil or imprudent means.

This is plainly stated in various places in *Sermons* 1–3: "whereas there is plainly benevolence or good-will, there is no such thing as love of injustice, oppression, treachery, ingratitude; but only eager desires after such and such external goods, which ... the most abandoned would choose to obtain by innocent means if they were as easy and as effectual to their end" (*S*. 1.12). "Several principles in the heart of man carry him to society, and to contribute to the happiness of it, in a sense and a manner in which no inward principle leads him to evil" (*S*. 2.2). These conclusions seem to follow, not from Butler's scrutiny of human nature, but from man's relation to

§ 3 · GOODNESS OF HUMAN NATURE

his maker. Every feature of human nature must have been constituted as it is for some good purpose.

But, as Butler recognises, we cannot plausibly explain away every kind of ill will as merely the pursuit of a good end by ill-chosen means, and nothing more. We have to admit that there is such a thing as pursuit of a malevolent end for its own sake. Butler meets this difficulty in his discussion of resentment, in *Sermons* 8 and 9. "Since no passion God hath endued us with can be in itself evil, and yet since men frequently indulge a passion in such ways and degrees that at length it becomes quite another thing from what it was originally in our nature – and those vices of malice and revenge in particular take their occasion from the natural passion of resentment – it will be needful to trace this up to its original, that we may see what it is in itself, as placed in our nature by its Author; from which it will plainly appear for what ends it was placed there" (*S*. 8.3).

Butler's solution is as follows. Resentment is of two kinds – impulsive or "sudden", and "deliberate". The first is evoked by sudden attack or opposition of any kind, and its final cause is self-defence: the second is evoked by wrong-doing, and its final cause is justice, the repression of wrong-doing, and the remedying of wrongs. But like any other passion it is open to abuse. The abuse of "sudden" resentment is seen in men of hot or peevish temper – those who rage or grumble when there is no occasion for self-defence. Deliberate resentment is abused when it is directed towards imagined or exaggerated injuries, or towards innocent occasions of injury, or when it is disproportionate to its occasion, "or lastly when pain or harm . . . is inflicted merely in consequence of, and to gratify, that resentment, though naturally raised" (*S*. 8.11).

This last clause reveals a very important confusion. Elsewhere, Butler gives the impression that every passion when "naturally" exercised – that is, when exercised in accordance with the highest principles in our nature – leads directly to some good end: its objective, that for the sake of which we act, is good. But resentment, according to the settled meaning of

[149]

the word, and according to Butler's description of it, is not the same thing as a desire for justice, the righting of wrongs, the preservation of life, and so on. "The cool consideration of reason, that the security and peace of society requires examples of justice should be made, might indeed be sufficient to procure laws to be enacted and sentence passed: but is it that cool reflection in the injured person which, for the most part, brings the offender to justice? or is it not resentment and indignation against the injury and the author of it?" (*S.* 8.14). Thus, Butler is able to reconcile the existence of resentment to the providential ordering of human nature only by showing that it may serve some end other than the end which the resentful person directly seeks as the objective of his resentment. And the working of resentment is only a second best means of compassing that end. It would be better if the final causes of resentment were always achieved as a result, not of resentment, but of benevolence and the desire to see justice done.

If Butler had recognised this consequence, he would have had to admit that there is such a thing as "real ill-will", even if it is providentially overruled for a good end. He could not have assumed that all passions are "naturally" good in the sense of having good objectives. He can, of course, continue to claim that they all have a place in the divine economy, and he would not have been disturbed by the argument that to promote good ends by second best means is a flaw in the divine economy. In reply he would have appealed to his doctrine of "the ignorance of man", set out in *Sermon* 15, and developed more fully in the *Analogy*. "The dealings of God with the children of men are not yet completed, and cannot be judged of by that part which is before us" (*S.* 15.6). "Our ignorance is the proper answer to many things which are called objections against religion; particularly to those which arise from the appearances of evil and irregularity in the constitution of nature and the government of the world. . . . From our ignorance of the constitution of things and the scheme of Providence in the government of the world; from

§ 3 · GOODNESS OF HUMAN NATURE

the reference the several parts have to each other, and to the whole; and from our not being able to see the end and the whole; it follows that, however perfect things are, they must even necessarily appear to us less perfect than they are" (*S.* 15.15).

These considerations leave undisturbed the whole of Butler's characteristic ethical teaching, resting on the empirical scrutiny of human nature. But in proportion as the ignorance of man is emphasised all attempts to connect knowledge of our duty with knowledge of final causes must become doubtful.

§ 4 · *The love of God*

A RIGHT action, in Butler's view, may be done from better or worse motives. We saw in the last section that order and security might be maintained, either from motives of benevolence and love of justice, or from revengeful feelings, kept within due bounds. "We may judge and determine that an action is morally good or evil, before we so much as consider whether it be interested or disinterested" (*Pr.* 39). And what is true of the interestedness or disinterestedness of motives is true of motives in general.

There is one possible motive of action which excels all others, and when we take it into account we see that Butler's autonomous and non-supernatural moral theory is incomplete. For even a right action conscientiously done is not as such in the highest class. Butler's teaching on this point is given most succinctly in *S.* 12.33. "That which we more strictly call piety, or the love of God, and which is an essential part of a right temper, some may perhaps imagine no way connected with benevolence: yet surely they must be connected; if there be indeed in being an object infinitely good. Human nature is so constituted that every good affection implies the love of itself; i.e. becomes the object of a new affection in the same person. Thus, to be righteous implies in it the love of righteousness;

[151]

to be benevolent the love of benevolence; to be good the love of goodness; whether this righteousness, benevolence, or goodness be viewed as in our own mind or in another's: and the love of God, as being perfectly good, is the love of perfect goodness contemplated in a being or person. Thus morality and religion, virtue and piety, will at last necessarily coincide, run up into one and the same point, and love will be in all senses 'the end of the commandment'."

In amplifying these ideas, Butler refers again to his doctrine that every "affection" "rests in its object as an end" (S. 13.5: see ch. 2, § 3), and that its object is "somewhat external". What is true of all affections is true of love; and what is true of love in general is true of the love of God.

We saw in chapter 2 that there is some confusion in this doctrine. When we speak of affections, passions, desires, and so on, common speech is, if not misleading, at least elliptical. We commonly think of the object of a desire as some more or less permanent thing or person. But more strictly what is desired is always some state of affairs – or a number of states of affairs – in which that person or thing plays a determinate part. In a society in which the institution of property is important, we are apt to think of ownership, or some relation analogous to ownership, as the normal or typical state of affairs which is desired. But a little reflection shows that ownership is seldom desired for its own sake, except by misers. We pass readily from "I desire X" to "I desire to have X", and *vice versa*, because we assume that ownership of X gives us the most absolute power of disposing of X which we can hope for. But ownership of money, for example, is not desired in the main for its own sake, but for the sake of spending money. The spending of money is desired for the sake of further ownership, and that in its turn is desired for the sake of various different enjoyments arising from the things money can buy.

Love between persons involves desires of two kinds: there is the desire for the well being of the loved person, and the desire to stand in a certain relation to the loved person – for

§ 4 · LOVE OF GOD

example, of companionship, or protection, or physical union. As everyone knows, both these kinds of desire are infinitely various, and love may take innumerable forms. But a disposition from which either of these kinds of desire was wholly absent could only be called love in a truncated sense. And it would not be proper to speak of love if desires of these kinds arose very fleetingly. The word 'love' stands for a continuant, not an occurrent passion.

Butler would not have denied what has just been said. He did not look beneath the elliptical idiom in which love is said to have a person as its object. But he implicitly recognises that the love of God contains, as parts, the desire that his will should be done – "our resignation to the will of God may be said to be perfect when our will is lost and resolved up into His" (*S.* 14.5); and the desire to enjoy whatever manner of society or union with him we may be capable of – "nothing is more certain than that an infinite being may Himself be, if He pleases, the supply to all the capacities of our nature" (*S.* 14.9).

The love of God is required by our nature. Without it we are incomplete and frustrated. "It is plain that there is a capacity in the nature of man which neither riches nor honours, nor sensual gratifications, nor anything in this world can perfectly fill up or satisfy: there is a deeper and more essential want than any of these things can be the supply of. Yet surely there is a possibility of somewhat which may fill up all our capacities of happiness; somewhat in which our souls may find rest; somewhat which may be to us that satisfactory good we are enquiring after. But it cannot be anything which is valuable only as it tends to some further end. Those, therefore, who have got this world so much into their hearts as not to be able to consider happiness as consisting in anything but property and possessions, which are only valuable as the means to somewhat else, cannot have the least glimpse of the subject before us, which is the end, not the means" (*S.* 14.9). And the love of God does not only supply a blank in our nature: it is due from us to our maker; it is the attitude morally

CH. 7 · GOD IN BUTLER'S ETHICS

fitting, on the part of such beings as ourselves, to such a being as God. "By the love of God I would understand all those regards ... which *are due* immediately to Him from such a creature as man" (*S.* 13.2 – my italics).

We see here the same kind of duality as appeared before in Butler's account of the relation between conscience and self-love. Just as morally right conduct is recommended to us in two ways – as what is binding on us, and as what will satisfy us most in the long run: so is the love of God, into which right conduct is supposed to be absorbed. There seems to be a problem here which Butler never resolved, though he was apparently quite undisturbed by it. We always feel some discomfort – at least outside the law courts – when a conclusion is recommended on two or more independent grounds, each of which should by itself be sufficient. Similarly, here it strikes us as an over lucky coincidence that the very same course of life which is binding on us should also be that which is most in our interest: or that the love of God should be, not only the sole means of fully satisfying the needs of our nature, but also something which is owing from us to God, to which he has a right. We have an uneasy feeling that the best is being made of both worlds somewhat too readily: that these recommendations stand on different footings, and that if we accept either of them as decisive we dismiss, by the same act, the point of view from which the other arises: that our obligations may in principle conflict with our interests, and if we recognise that we are under obligations any reference to our interests is overruled; while if, on the other hand, we commit ourselves to seeking the most complete satisfaction, we are rejecting the idea of obligation.

For Butler, as is implied in the passage quoted above from *S.* 12.33, the coincidence of obligation and interest is, not lucky, but providential. But it follows that, for those who do not accept his theological premises, his ethical teaching must contain a lacuna. If we are satisfied, from our knowledge of God's goodness and power, that obligation and interest really do coincide, we may be content to dismiss intellectual puzzles

§ 4 · LOVE OF GOD

as to which of the two has a prepotent claim. But if we wish for an ethical system standing on its own feet, we cannot dismiss the question how obligation and interest are related. In chapter 3 it was argued that Butler decided the question in favour of obligation. No other interpretation seems to make sense of his insistence on the authority of conscience. Yet if there are obligations, capable in principle of overriding our interests, why is the appeal to self-love so much stressed? The reason is, perhaps, that Butler has conflated two distinct assertions. He wishes to refute, on solid empirical grounds, the vulgar errors and philosophical sophistries according to which there is a necessary and universal conflict between duty and interest, so that whenever I do what I ought to do it follows that I am doing what is against my interests. But he held also, on theological grounds, that on the whole and in the long run duty and interest coincide completely. He did not sufficiently distinguish the two propositions: (1) that my obligations do not always conflict with my interests; and (2) that my obligations always coincide with my interests. In order to "obviate that scorn which one sees rising upon the faces of people who are said to know the world, when mention is made of a disinterested, generous, or public-spirited action" (*Pr.* 38) it was the first proposition which had to be insisted on. But Butler commonly goes beyond it, and insists on the second. Now from the second proposition the first follows: but the stronger claim which the second makes is harder to sustain. It is easy enough to show, and Butler does show, that there are instances of public-spirited action; and that such actions are not always against the interests of those who do them. But it is much harder to show that they are never against their interests, and Butler tacitly admits (*S.* 3.8) that this cannot be proved solely on empirical grounds drawn from observation of human life in this world. To be assured of the second proposition we need to know man's ultimate destiny.

One point in Butler's teaching about the love of God is difficult to interpret. In several places he lays stress on the

CH. 7 · GOD IN BUTLER'S ETHICS

principle that "every good affection implies the love of itself": "to be a just, a good, a righteous man plainly carries with it a peculiar affection to or love of justice, goodness, righteousness, when these principles are the objects of contemplation" (*S*. 13.7). Since Butler adds that this affection "cannot but be in those who have any degree of real goodness in themselves, and who discern and take notice of the same principle in others", we may take it that the secondary affection is directed to other persons who possess good qualities: we are not concerned here with any affection which might be excited by the contemplation of justice, say, in the abstract – even if, what there is no reason to suppose Butler believed, it is intelligible to speak of affection for a quality contemplated in the abstract.

Butler's principle seems susceptible of at least two interpretations, and it is hard to be sure which Butler would have accepted. It might be meant that the concept of, say, a just character contains two parts: a man is just if, in the first place, he tends to act justly, and to be moved by the thought of justice on suitable occasions; and secondly he feels affection or approval for other people of similar disposition. This would presuppose that we can distinguish an elementary sense of the word 'just', in which a particular transaction, such as the paying of a debt, may be called just: and a more complex derivative sense in which a person's character may be called just, definable in terms of the elementary sense of the word. If this were what Butler meant, it would be quite plausible. If a man acted justly or benevolently, and yet there was no distinction between his sentiments and attitudes towards other people, according as they were or were not just or benevolent, we should feel that the benevolence or justice of his own character was somehow incomplete. But on this interpretation Butler's principle would be a tautology, derived from the definition of 'just' or 'benevolent' when those words are applied to a man's character: a good quality implies the love of itself, because in the absence of the secondary affection the name of the good quality will not be applicable. Since God is perfectly good, it

[156]

§ 4 · LOVE OF GOD

follows that no one who is aware of God's goodness without feeling any love for God can be said to have a good character. But this conclusion does not help to show, either that the love of God supplies a need of man's nature, or that love is due from man to God. For the first conclusion we need empirical evidence about human nature: and for the second we need independent moral insight into the proper relations between such a being as man and such a being as God.

The other interpretation which suggests itself is empirical. Butler might claim that, in actual fact, men are so constituted that, whenever they are just or benevolent, they always, on reflection, find themselves kindly disposed towards those who are just or benevolent. It is hard to see how Butler could really be sure about this claim, as a universal generalisation, unless it borrowed some factitious support from the tautology with which it might be confused: just as people often feel that it is intuitively certain that parallel lines could never meet, however far produced, because we sometimes make never meeting part of the meaning of the word 'parallel'. But even if the generalisation were true, its relation to Butler's teaching about the love of God is rather obscure. Butler holds, as we have seen, that unless men love God wholeheartedly the deepest needs of their nature will be unsatisfied: and also that love is morally due from men to God. Both these contentions imply that the love of God has to be recommended to men; that without adequate insight into their own nature and their obligations men might fail to love God. But if it is universally true that good affections imply love of themselves, good men who recognise God's existence and his perfect goodness will always necessarily love God; though bad men may not. And bad men may be led to love God by being led to improve their own characters: if they cultivate the good elements in their own nature the rest will follow.

It seems, then, that Butler had not thought out very fully the implications of this principle. The rest of his teaching seems to suppose that a man might be, in other respects, well-intentioned and conscientious, and yet might fail to recognise the special place which God ought to hold in his affections. But if it were true that every good quality of character always carries with it the love of itself, a good man who was a believer in God's goodness could not be in need of any further enlightenment.

CHAPTER 8

SOME ULTIMATE PROBLEMS OF ETHICS

§ 1 · *The idea of obligation*

IN the preceding chapters, the idea of obligation has been used uncritically. It has been tacitly supposed that obligation is *sui generis*, and not analysable: and some proposed analyses – for instance, that to be obliged is to be commanded by God – have been rejected. This seems to have been Butler's assumption (*Pr.* 26–29). Yet, in discussing Shaftesbury's views, he says, "interest, one's own happiness, is a manifest obligation". Again (*S.* 3.5) "your obligation to obey this law" (the moral law) "is its being the law of your nature". This language suggests, though it does not entail, that obligation is *identified* with some natural need or want of a human person, or with the satisfying of it: that the statement 'I am under an obligation to do X' means exactly the same as some statement that to do X will be an exercise of some *nisus* within me, or will bring me nearer to some goal at which I am in fact aiming. This is vague, and we need not, for the purpose of our present discussion, decide between the various more definite forms which such a doctrine might take. They would consist of identifying particular obligations with "passions", or with dominant passions, or with their satisfaction; or identifying obligation in general with self-love, or with the most comprehensive satisfaction of passions.

Most moral philosophers would maintain that any theory of this type is completely mistaken. The mistake can be most readily seen if we reflect that, about any course of action dictated by self-love, or by some passion or combination of passions, it is always significant to ask 'am I obliged to act in this way?', or again, 'shall I be infringing some obligation by acting in this way?'. If obligation were to be identified with self-love or some passion or combination of passions, such questions would be trifling: we should be asking some such question as 'is the course of action prescribed by self-love the course of action prescribed by self-love?'. And it seems clear that the type of question instanced never reduces itself to this trifling form. Even if, as Butler sometimes hints, what I am under an obligation to do always coincides with what it is in my best interests to do, the statement of this coincidence would be a synthetic statement, not a tautology: it would be a statement to the effect that two distinct characteristics, obligatoriness and advantageousness, belong to the same course of action.

Butler's language does not always exclude this mistaken analysis of obligation, but neither is he committed to it. When he speaks of "*that authority and obligation* which is a constituent part of... reflex approbation" (*Pr.* 27 – my italics), he suggests a different view. As has already been argued in a different connection (ch. 4, § 5), Butler's insistence on the authority of conscience would be pointless if "self-love" and "conscience" were merely two names for the same principle. It is by conscientious reflection, not by prudence, that obligations are discerned, and the distinction between conscience and self-love would disappear unless conscientious reflection had this distinct subject matter to exercise itself upon: what my obligations are, not what will pay me best.

The same point may be put in another form in the terminology used in ch. 3, § 3. To assert an obligation is, not merely to give a reason for acting in a certain way, but to give a prepotent reason, which, as such, overrules reasons of an inferior kind.

When Butler speaks of one's own happiness as "a manifest obligation", or says that our obligation to obey a law "*is* its being the law of your nature" (my italics), the only tolerable interpretation of his words is that he is not outlining an analysis of the idea of obligation, but is setting out some of

§ 1 · IDEA OF OBLIGATION

the value-bearing, or 'obligation-bearing' qualities upon which the existence of an obligation depends. This is illustrated in the discussion of forgiveness (*S.* 9.15): in the course of opposing the assertion that a man's bad character may annul all duties of good will towards him, Butler writes "it is not man's being a social creature, much less his being a moral agent, from whence *alone* our obligations of good-will towards him arise. There is an obligation to it prior to either of these, arising from his being a sensible creature; that is, capable of happiness or misery. Now this obligation cannot be superseded by his moral character."

In other words, determinate kinds of existing things, and the determinate relations in which they stand, generate obligations of a determinate kind: these obligations are found out by "reflection". For example, by reflecting on the nature of anything capable of happiness or misery we discern an obligation upon ourselves to spare that thing misery and procure it happiness, so far as we have the opportunity. But this is only one obligation among many, and one obligation may override another. To pursue Butler's own example, in the passage just referred to, if a criminal has to be punished for "the quiet and happiness of the world ... a general and more enlarged obligation necessarily destroys a particular and more confined one of the same kind, inconsistent with it". The word "destroy" is perhaps not happily chosen: for Butler would probably not mean to claim that moral obligations on the part of a judge towards a felon are totally abolished. But what is meant to be expressed is rather that a situation exists – as such situations may often exist – in which there are incompatible obligations: and in such situations we have to discover which is of highest authority.

There is a certain clumsiness of language in our description of these situations: for the statement 'you are under an obligation to do X' might be taken to mean that X is what is morally required of you, and that no other claim upon you can take away this obligation; or it might be taken as compatible with 'you are under an obligation to do Y', when X and Y are

CH. 8 · ULTIMATE PROBLEMS OF ETHICS

incompatible with one another, so that we cannot mean to say that both X and Y are morally required. Modern writers, in particular Sir David Ross, have introduced a special terminology to avoid confusion between these two senses of such words as 'obligation'. They propose that, when by saying that I am under an obligation to do X we do not exclude my being also under an obligation to do Y, which is incompatible with X, we shall speak of the relation in which I am supposed to stand to X and Y as a "*prima facie* obligation", or "conditional obligation". But when the statement that I am under an obligation to do X means that X is morally required of me, and no competing claim can interfere, we are to say without qualification that to do X is an obligation, or perhaps that it is a categorical obligation. In this way we can mark systematically the distinction Butler refers to when he speaks of one obligation "superseding" another.

§ 2 · *Naturalistic and non-naturalistic ethics*

A CLEAR statement of the conception of obligation as *sui generis* allows us to formulate accurately the distinction between what modern writers call "naturalistic" and "non-naturalistic" ethical theories. If there are categorical obligations, and if no statement that a categorical obligation exists can be resolved into statements about obligation-bearing qualities; and if, further, no amount of knowledge about obligation-bearing qualities would, by itself, tell us what our obligations were; it follows that knowledge of obligations – supposing that we can know them – must be obtained by some quite distinct process, different from any process by which we get to know the facts of the physical world, or human history, or human psychology. If that is the case, as non-naturalists in ethics hold, moral judgements form a self-contained system. They do not overlap, or merge into, judgements about matters of fact, but are totally distinct. They involve perhaps one concept, such as that of obligation, or

§ 2 · NATURALISTIC AND NON-NATURALISTIC

perhaps several, which do not occur in any other kind of judgement: and the applicability of this concept, or these concepts, can only be known by some distinctive method. Naturalists in ethics, on the other hand, hold that there is no sharp division between ordinary judgements of fact, and the concepts they involve, and judgements about, for example, obligation.

The general issue between naturalists and non-naturalists is still hotly debated, and we cannot hope to settle the question here. But something may be said of the strong and weak points of the two sides, as illustrated by the notion of obligation.

A non-naturalistic position, suitably formulated, seems to answer very exactly to our established ways of expressing our judgements about conduct. When we ask ourselves whether a course of action is right or wrong, whether or not we are under an obligation, whether an aim is good, bad or indifferent, and when, on the other hand, we ask ourselves whether an aim or course of action is satisfying, or profitable, either to one person or to many, we have a strong impression that the first kind of question stands on its own feet. The answer to the second kind of question contributes to our power of answering the first: but it does not by itself provide an answer. It may or may not be true – Butler doubted whether it was, but some non-naturalists have held the contrary – that general tests of the rightness of an action can be found. But even if they can, rightness and wrongness do not resolve themselves into the tests of rightness and wrongness. It may be true, for instance, that an action is right if, and only if, it has at least as much tendency to produce happiness as any other action would have had. But its rightness is not to be identified with its tendency to produce happiness. Similarly, if I am under an obligation to keep a promise, it may be that the obligation arises from the fact that the habit of promise-keeping is useful: but the fact that I am under the obligation is distinct from the fact that my keeping the promise will have certain useful effects.

To this, a naturalist might reply that people undoubtedly

CH. 8 · ULTIMATE PROBLEMS OF ETHICS

have certain distinctive *feelings*, which we may call feelings of obligation; and that to have a feeling of obligation towards a certain course of action is undoubtedly different from merely feeling attracted to it in some way – that feelings of obligation may, indeed, conflict very sharply with inclinations. But, they would add, there is no strong reason to regard these feelings as of much importance in distinguishing between good and bad conduct. On the contrary, the modern psychology of the unconscious may be held to have shown that these feelings are generated by inner conflicts set up through a person's relations with his parents and others very early in life. If we succeed in bringing the sources of these feelings under conscious scrutiny we often have to recognise that there is no good reason to be guided by them, and the feelings themselves often tend to fade away, or to be redistributed.

Secondly, a naturalist might say, there are obligations proper, namely requirements imposed on us by law, by engagements voluntarily entered into, and by services rendered by one person to another. There is no logical connection between having a feeling of obligation and being under an obligation in the sense now pointed out. But the use of the same name in both connections is appropriate because legal and contractual obligations, and debts of gratitude, tend to produce feelings of obligation. Now obligations in this sense are not the same thing as moral obligations: we tend to think that as a rule the law should be obeyed, engagements should be kept, and gratitude should be shown to benefactors. But we also think that this rule has exceptions. Unjust and oppressive laws should sometimes be broken, and other duties may override the keeping of contracts or paying of debts of gratitude.

What, then, is a moral obligation? According to the naturalistic view we are sketching the idea of moral obligation, and the related idea of a moral law, is confused. Any determinate obligation, in the non-moral sense of the word, implies a more or less definite and circumscribed course of action, by which the obligation is to be fulfilled – the paying of a tax, for example, or the keeping of an appointment. And there is a fairly well defined procedure for ascertaining whether an obligation of this nature exists; for example, by looking up the Finance Act, or consulting an engagement book. In a great many cases, we regard non-moral obligations uncritically: we rely on the general presumption in favour of obeying the law, keeping promises, and so on, and we therefore accept the limited procedure of ascertaining a non-moral obligation as completely settling the question how we should act.

When we think about moral obligations, and suppose them to be applications of a moral law, we wrongly assume that there is some equivalent of this simple limited procedure, by means of which every moral question can be settled. But once there is a conflict between non-moral obligations, or between obligation and inclination, or once we come to question the rightness of discharging a particular non-moral obligation, that is not the case.

The sphere of non-moral obligations may be compared with a well mapped countryside, with clearly defined roads and easily recognised natural features, over which we can find our way simply by map reading. To suppose that all moral questions can be settled by some process comparable to finding out the law is rather like supposing that all countries are mapped, all maps are accurate, and all landscapes contain landmarks. Or, to elaborate the illustration a little more, the assumption that we can settle all moral questions by the exercise of a special faculty, conscience, which discerns a moral law, is rather like the assumption that, in the absence of physical maps, we can find our way by means of a special map-reading faculty which is exercised upon invisible maps.

This is the mistake made by non-naturalists in ethics, when they assume the existence of moral obligations and a moral law. Of course, it would be going much too far to argue that every use of such words as 'obligation' and 'law' in an ethical connection is confused. But the use of these words tends to suggest a non-existent precision and definiteness as belonging to the process of deciding how we should act.

These considerations would be enforced by pointing to notorious instances of the diversity of conscience. Not only are there great differences between the prevailing moral judgements of different ages and places – Butler was wrong in supposing that there is a "standard of virtue ... which all ages and all countries have made profession of in public" (*D. on V.* 1): but the lack of agreement among moral philosophers themselves goes to refute the view that there is a distinct kind of moral law knowable by a distinct faculty.

We have sketched a naturalistic attack on a non-naturalistic theory of obligation. There are, of course, other forms of non-naturalism, which make, not obligation, but goodness or intrinsic value the fundamental ethical notion. Naturalistic criticism of these views would have to be differently formulated. But the general objection would remain, that if we cannot recognise a distinct realm of moral truths, and a distinct power within ourselves of apprehending such truths, non-naturalists have no arguments to make us do so. For Butler obligation is the fundamental notion, and we may therefore content ourselves with discussing the issue between naturalists and non-naturalists in terms of obligation.

But what is the alternative? a non-naturalist might reply. If you do not recognise any distinctive concept, such as that of obligation, which is *sui generis*, and which we discern the application of by some distinctive faculty, how do you distinguish moral judgements from others? And if there is no distinction between moral judgements and others, or only a vague and loose distinction, how can there be such a subject as ethics at all? If the ideas of obligation, moral law, right and wrong, good and bad, are all to be resolved into the ideas of, let us say, feelings of approval and disapproval, or of the satisfying and frustrating of desire, moral philosophy becomes a vaguely defined, and amateurishly practised, subsection of sociology, or psychology.

To this some naturalists would reply that they accept the

§ 2 · NATURALISTIC AND NON-NATURALISTIC

conclusion that ethics is not a clearly defined and autonomous study. Its unity, they would say, is historical: there is a long tradition, in philosophy and theology, according to which the valuation of human conduct is a quite distinct branch of knowledge. But the position of a naturalistic moral philosopher is transitional: his task is to show that the traditional tangle of problems *can* be resolved into questions about human desires and feelings and men's social relations; and he will be quite content if, as a result of his efforts, the traditional discipline known as 'ethics' disappears.

§ 3 · *What is a moral judgement?*

CAN we distinguish a well defined class of judgements or attitudes, which have some common and peculiar characteristic besides that of being generally named 'moral'? And can we mark off moral judgements from others in terms which are neutral towards all ethical theories, which do not, for example, presuppose either a naturalistic or a non-naturalistic type of theory? One might expect to find the answer to these questions in the first chapter of any ethical treatise. But most moral philosophers do not seem to have attempted an answer.

The most obvious statement of the content of an ethical treatise would be to the effect that it is concerned with certain ideas, for instance the idea of duty, or obligation, or goodness, or value, and with the truths, or judgements, or statements, in which those ideas occur, for example rules of conduct or statements of ideals. But as to the content of those ideas, and those judgements – or, to put the point more radically, as to the meaning of such words as 'good' or 'duty', moral philosophers disagree. It is at this very stage, where the subject-matter of ethics has to be specified, that opposing ethical schools part company. In the eyes of non-naturalists, as we have seen, there is a distinct concept, or class of concepts, which is what we mean by the word 'good', or the word

[167]

'right', or the word 'duty', which cannot be analysed, and moral judgements and moral truths may be defined as consisting of all the judgements or truths which involve that concept, or a concept of that class, and of those judgements only. For non-naturalists, therefore, there is a distinct object for systematic study sharply separated from all other classes of concepts and classes of judgements, and the name 'ethics' can be given a precise sense. But it follows, unfortunately, that the specification of his subject-matter which a non-naturalist would give must necessarily be unacceptable to a naturalist, and may well be unacceptable to a non-naturalist of a different persuasion: for if, for example, one theorist holds that the topic he is dealing with is a certain unanalysable quality whose name is 'goodness', he will be defining his subject in a way which cannot be accepted by a theorist who claims to be dealing with an unanalysable concept whose name is 'duty', and who analyses goodness in terms of duty.

A naturalistic theorist holds, as we have seen, that there is no unanalysable idea whatever which is peculiar to moral judgements. The names 'good', 'duty', and so on, which are commonly held to stand for the peculiar ethical subject-matter, all stand for psychological or sociological concepts: they refer in some way to human desires or fears, human happiness or unhappiness, the evolution and structure of human society, or something of that sort. And it is obvious that we make many judgements with this sort of content which would never strike anyone as belonging to the class of moral judgements. So, as we have seen, a consistent naturalist may well be obliged to admit that the subject he is dealing with is a somewhat miscellaneous and haphazard selection from the total range of psychological and sociological judgements. A non-naturalist, in his view, is asserting the existence of a spurious unity in this haphazard selection. Non-naturalists suppose that ethics differs from other subjects as sharply as, say, geometry differs from arithmetic; whereas really it differs only as school arithmetic differs from arithmetic in general.

We cannot, a radical naturalist might continue, distinguish

§ 3 · WHAT IS A MORAL JUDGEMENT?

moral judgements from others in any systematic way, except by saying that they are judgements expressed by means of certain specified words – words which may even have no counterparts in some languages.

It has often been pointed out that the matters in which moral philosophers have been interested cannot in fact be adequately delimited in terms of the words 'good', 'wrong', 'duty', and so on, because these words have non-ethical as well as ethical uses, and all moral philosophers would agree in setting aside the non-ethical uses, and confining their attention to whatever these words express in their ethical uses. When we speak of 'a good drainage system' or 'a wrong turning' or 'the duties of a goal-keeper' we are not expressing the sort of judgement with which moral philosophers are concerned. It seems to follow that all parties can recognise some distinct type of meaning which they discern as belonging to those words in some of their uses only, and that the extreme naturalist position we have been developing must be mistaken.

But it might be replied that we draw this distinction by reference to the choices we happen to think momentous and trivial. Naturalists and non-naturalists, at least if they are contemporaries speaking the same language, inherit a common set of moral ideas. They therefore agree quite well in drawing a line between ethical and non-ethical uses of words, or moral and non-moral judgements, because they accept more or less the same traditional assumptions as to what is worth making a fuss about.

Enough has perhaps been said to show that the answer to the question with which this section opened is not obvious. The question was whether we can find any method of defining a moral judgement which will not presuppose any ethical theory, and which will be neutral as between naturalism and non-naturalism. The definition required will not be an exact account of the actual usage of the phrase 'moral judgement': that is too fluid to be represented by a single precise formula. But it should correspond to ordinary usage, or at least the usage of theorists, to the extent that nearly all the things

CH. 8 · ULTIMATE PROBLEMS OF ETHICS

which fall under the definition would be commonly recognised as moral judgements, and few things excluded by it would be so recognised.

We may proceed by setting out what seem to be necessary conditions of its being true, of any person, that he makes a moral judgement.

1. In the first place no one can be said to make a moral judgement unless he stands in some relation to a certain action, or type of conduct, or the pursuit of a certain end: and the relation in which he stands must be other than *doing* that action, or an action of that type, or *pursuing* that end. The relation is one of being, in some way, favourably, or unfavourably, disposed towards that action, or class of actions, or end. Thus, there is no reason why those who make moral judgements about lying or stealing should themselves lie or steal – nor yet why they should themselves avoid lying and stealing. The doing of the action, or the avoidance of it, and the making of moral judgements about it, are logically independent of one another. But a man who makes a moral judgement about lying and stealing must have an attitude of some kind to those types of action: and the attitude must include a tendency to favour and promote, or else a tendency to condemn and oppose, that kind of action.

A favourable or unfavourable attitude to an action may be strong or weak. Its strength or weakness may be measured in a rough and ready way by the amount of trouble to which a man is prepared to go in order to bring about or prevent the action in question. In a more exact account of the strength of an attitude, we should have to take note of the fact that people may be favourably or unfavourably disposed, not only towards actions which fall within their range of influence, but equally towards actions in the remote past, or on the part of imaginary characters. But it is comparatively easy to extend the notion of strength, by analogy, to these cases, as will shortly be shown. The attitudes with which we are concerned may vary, then, in at least three respects: in respect of the action, or class of actions, or end, towards which the attitude is directed,

§ 3 · WHAT IS A MORAL JUDGEMENT?

which may be called its 'goal'; in respect of being favourable or unfavourable, which may be called the 'direction' of the attitude; and in respect of strength.

2. Secondly, a man cannot be said to make a moral judgement unless the attitude we have spoken of remains unchanged in direction, and more or less unchanged in strength, whoever may be supposed to do the action, or pursue the end, which forms the goal of the attitude. Thus, if a man were favourably disposed towards lying on the part of himself and his friends, but unfavourably disposed towards lying on the part of his enemies, he could not be said to be making a moral judgement about lying. This condition may be expressed by saying that, in order that he shall be said to make a moral judgement, his attitude must be 'universalisable'.

This does not imply, of course, that every moral judgement must involve the wholesale approval or condemnation of some widely defined class of actions. It is commonly held, for example, that lying should in general be avoided, but is morally allowable in some circumstances. But if I take that view, my condemnation of lying is not for that reason not universalisable. Suppose, for the sake of illustration, that the only exception I make is in favour of lying to save someone's life. My attitude is universalisable, provided I favour acts of lying for the saving of life, and condemn other acts of lying, no matter by whom they are done.

It may also happen that the action or pursuit to which a moral judgement relates is qualified, not, or not only, in respect of varying circumstances or effects, but in respect of varying capacities on the part of the agent. Thus we might think it incumbent on a good swimmer to try to rescue a drowning man, but not on a non-swimmer; we might hold that a musical genius was under an obligation to cultivate his musical gifts, but that people of average musical ability were under no such obligation. The attitude answering to such moral judgements as these would be universalisable, provided it remained unchanged in direction and strength no matter who the swimmer or the musical genius might be.

CH. 8 · ULTIMATE PROBLEMS OF ETHICS

To sum up the second condition, a man cannot be making a moral judgement unless his attitude is free from partiality for particular places, ages, and social groups, and from self-partiality: or rather, since men are very local and self-partial beings, and since we do not wish to define a moral judgement so stringently as to entail that no moral judgements are ever made, the attitude must be at least *relatively* free from those partialities. This means that if, for instance, a man strongly condemns lying on the part of his enemies, but condemns similar lying on the part of himself or his friends rather less strongly, we shall not on that account deny that he is making a moral judgement about lying. He may still be making a moral judgement, provided that the direction of his attitude is unchanged, and the variation in strength is not excessive. It follows, of course, that the notion of a moral judgement is inherently vague – since we cannot specify what degree of variation in strength is supposed to be tolerable – but this seems inevitable. If we wished to be more precise, we might say that the applicability of the notion of a moral judgement varies in degree. The notion is fully applicable only if the attitude concerned never varies in strength: the notion is partly applicable, to a varying degree, in proportion as the strength of the attitude concerned varies much or little.

It would sometimes be hard in practice to determine how far someone's attitude was vitiated by partiality, and so not universalisable. For there is partiality of cognition as well as of feeling. A man might genuinely fail to discern characteristics in himself and his friends which he saw quite clearly in other people: and he might put harsh and false constructions upon the conduct of his enemies. In that case, although his attitude would be based on misjudgements of fact, it might still be universalisable in so far as he was reacting in the same way to what he supposed to be the same types of conduct. Butler would probably hold that mistakes of this kind proceed from "falseness of heart" – see *Sermons* 9 and 10 – and are not mere intellectual errors, but faults of character. We need not decide the difficult question, how far mistakes of this

§ 3 · WHAT IS A MORAL JUDGEMENT?

nature may be morally innocent. In so far as they were not, an attitude influenced by such a mistake could not properly be called universalisable, because the mistake would itself be a consequence of partial attitudes. The difficulties of fathoming the human heart do not make the notion of universalisability any less intelligible, but only harder to apply.

It is not implied that, when a man's attitude is of the kind we are describing, he consciously universalises it by contemplating a variety of people and situations and responding in an equivalent way to all of them. What we are calling the universalisability of his attitude consists in his being disposed, having a tendency, to respond in an equivalent way to people and situations of a given kind, should he come to consider them.

We defined the strength of an attitude in terms of a man's readiness to put himself out in order to promote or hinder actions of a certain class. Now that the condition of universalisability has been added we can see that there is no difficulty about calling an attitude strong or weak, even when it is directed to remote or imaginary conduct. For a man's attitude to Caesar crossing the Rubicon, or Anna Karenina leaving her husband, will not satisfy our second condition unless he responds in a corresponding way to similar conquerors, or similar unhappy wives, wherever they may be placed. And the strength of his attitude is measured by the amount of trouble he would be prepared to take, if a case of the relevant kind came within reach of his own influence.

It will be noticed that we have already delimited the scope of the term 'moral judgement' in such a way as to exclude some attitudes to which the name 'moral' is sometimes given. We have excluded what is sometimes called 'tribal morality': that is, if a man favours a given type of action when it is done by a member of a certain class, or totem, or a person with a skin of a certain colour, but condemns actions of the same type when they are done by someone of a different class, totem, or skin colour – however consistent he may be in the application of his tribal rules – his attitude will not fulfil the conditions of universalisability.

CH. 8 · ULTIMATE PROBLEMS OF ETHICS

This point needs one qualification, which is not important in principle, but in whose absence there might be misunderstanding. We can imagine that, for the performing of some task or other, membership of a certain race or social group might be an indispensable precondition. Let us suppose, for instance, that a person of nervous temper and limited views has to have medical attention. It is supposable that such a person might be upset, alarmed, and injured in health, by the attentions of a doctor of alien race and culture. In such circumstances, we may be in favour of the patient being attended by any doctor of race *A*, but against the attendance of any doctor of race *B*. The distinction we draw here is obviously akin to the distinction we might draw, in other situations, between the duties of swimmers and non-swimmers, or between the duties of those who are musically gifted and those who are not. We draw the distinction according as we foresee success or failure, in performing a certain task, on the part of someone qualified in a certain way. If our attitude is to be described as universalisable in any one of these cases, it must be so described in the others.

What is excluded, then, by the condition of universalisability? It excludes only those attitudes which vary according to race, place, time, and so on, without reference to any further effects which a person's actions might have because he is acting under certain social conditions or in a certain age and place. In modern times, of course, tribal moralities tend to disguise themselves *sub specie universalis*. When a Jewish doctor is forbidden to attend Gentile patients, or when a person of capitalist origins is forbidden to manage a factory, it is usually claimed that some distinctive vice inheres in the so called Jewish race, or in a capitalist background, which prevents the persons in question from achieving the same results as would be achieved by a similarly qualified Gentile or proletarian. We see here again the practical difficulty, already noticed, of discovering how far a certain attitude on the part of a certain person is universalisable.

3. Thirdly, a man cannot be said to make a moral judgement

[174]

§ 3 · WHAT IS A MORAL JUDGEMENT?

unless his attitude remains unchanged in direction, and relatively unchanged in strength, towards his own conduct, even when it conflicts with his inclinations, or with prudent pursuit of his own interests. Briefly, the attitude of which we have spoken stands in potential opposition to self-love. Given that an attitude is universalisable, it follows that it may be extended to actions on one's own part: if a man discountenances lying by other people, but approves of any lies he himself feels inclined to tell, his attitude is not universalisable. But because an attitude extends to the possessor of the attitude, it does not follow that it conflicts with self-love. Self-love itself is universalised, if I approve or condemn everyone's conduct, including my own, according as it contributes to or lessens *my* well-being. And apart from that limiting case, it is conceivable that someone's attitude to a certain class of conduct should be universalisable, and yet always in harmony with his own inclinations and interests. For example, a man of preternaturally even temper might universally condemn outbursts of anger. This third characteristic is, therefore, not a mere consequence of universalisability. Given that people are what they are, it may be that every universalisable attitude *does* tend to conflict with self-love: opposition between self-love and conscience is certainly a marked feature of what is commonly regarded as moral judging. That might be a sufficient reason for stressing the third condition. However, it has to be stated separately, not for that reason, but because it is logically independent of universalisability.

Without doing much violence to the meanings of words, we may hold that any state of mind which is to be called a moral judgement must fulfil the three foregoing conditions. But if we went on to maintain that these conditions are, not only necessary, but jointly sufficient to constitute a moral judgement – that they are defining conditions, so that if anyone fulfils them it *follows*, without any further grounds being needed, that he is making a moral judgement – if we maintained that, a strong objection would be felt. For surely the making of a moral judgement must be a cognitive state – it must be, or at least it must include, some species of thinking or reflecting or perceiving or knowing, having as its object some kind of truth, or fact, or proposition, or actual or possible state of affairs. But in our three conditions nothing of that kind has been mentioned. All that has been mentioned is tendencies to feel and act.

Now it may well be admitted that any state of mind fulfilling our three conditions – which for the moment may be called a 'moral disposition' – contains some cognitive element. And it may be supposed – though this is controvertible – that every moral disposition contains some distinctive cognitive element, common and peculiar to moral dispositions, present in all of them, and never found in the absence of a moral disposition. But there is no agreement among moral philosophers as to what this cognitive element may be: and in view of the considerations raised at the beginning of the present section, it is hard to see how there could be agreement, until all ethical controversy had ceased. It would therefore be a substantial gain if moral philosophers would accept something like the foregoing definition of a moral disposition as giving the meaning of the phrase 'moral judgement'. The controversies between them could then be formulated, not as disagreements about what a moral judgement is, but as disagreements about the further characteristics, if any, which belong to moral judgements, over and above those specified in the definition.

Where we have used the phrase 'moral judgement' Butler would have used some such phrase as "the determination, or sentence, of conscience". The drawback of Butler's terminology, as coloured by Butler's exposition, is that it carries a strong suggestion that the word "conscience" is used in what we have called a 'Kantian' sense (ch. 3, § 6). But it is desirable to use a terminology which will leave open the possibility that, in spite of Kant and Butler, a conscientious or quasi-conscientious attitude may be mistaken. While there is always a certain air of paradox about the supposition that a man may follow his conscience and yet be in the wrong, there is no such paradox in the supposition that, among moral

§ 3 · WHAT IS A MORAL JUDGEMENT?

judgements, some may be true and some false; or some wise and some foolish.

In what follows, the phrase 'moral judgement' will be used to mean no less and no more than what we have meant by the phrase 'moral disposition'; that is, a man will be held to make a moral judgement if he fulfils the three conditions we have expounded. We shall deliberately leave open the question whether moral judgements *are*, in the most familiar sense, judgements at all – whether they are cognitive attitudes; or whether they are judgements only in a Pickwickian sense, like that in which Prairie Oysters are oysters. This may seem to be a piece of wilfully perverse terminology: but it can be justified. It could, as was said above, most probably be agreed by all parties that the existence of a moral disposition is at least a necessary condition of the existence of a moral judgement; or, to put the point a little more loosely, that nearly all, if not all, the states of mind commonly called moral judgements fall under our definition. But as soon as we attempt to add any description of the cognitive side of these states of mind, we fall among the well-known controversies between ethical sensationalists, intuitionists, rationalists, emotionalists, and so on. It is a matter of dispute whether moral judgements are something like states of sense perception, or like recognition of mathematical truths, or like deductions from generalisations, or like awareness of one's own feelings, or of some other nature: and there are corresponding disputes about the character of the propositions or facts with which the judgements are concerned. Thus, at the expense of a definition which is at first glance paradoxical, we gain a neutral terminology, which can be used by all parties to refer to the matters on which their disputes turn.

Butler would certainly recognise what we are calling a moral judgement as forming part of a "determination of conscience". The first condition, and perhaps the third, may be collected from his express statements: we have a "moral approving and disapproving faculty" which is directed towards "actions and characters" (*D. on V.* 1): and that this faculty is distinct from particular passions and self-love is shown at length in the *Preface* and the first three *Sermons*. The second condition, universalisability, is never stated so plainly by Butler. The reason for this is that, as has been argued in ch. 3, § 1, Butler never seriously questioned the principles of the uniformity of duty and the uniformity of conscience. From these it follows that whatever any man, in the exercise of conscience, sees to be his duty, would also be the duty of any other man whatever, similarly qualified and similarly situated. And if a man failed to see that that was the case – if he supposed his own duties to be at variance with other people's, so that his attitude was not universalisable – he would not be properly and candidly exercising his conscience: he would be influenced by self-partiality or corruptness of heart. Thus, the condition of universalisability is implicit in Butler's account of conscience.

Yet, unless our exposition in ch. 3 is completely misconceived, Butler would have had to hold that a moral judgement is only part of a determination of conscience. Our notion of a moral judgement answers quite adequately to that aspect of conscience, in Butler, in which it is described as a "sentiment", and is connected with the "heart": but nothing has been said of any cognitive aspect, its being a "perception", in Butler's language, or connected with the "understanding". There are moral qualities whose inherence in good and bad actions and characters is "prior to all will whatever". And in the exercise of conscience we discern those qualities, and our moral inclinations depend on our discernment of them.

§ 4 · *Man's aptitude for virtue*

IN ch. 3, §§ 4–5, we sought to restate Butler's view of the cognitive part of a moral judgement. We suggested that the moral qualities of actions and ends might have a distinctive characteristic, 'intrinsic stringency', in virtue of which the presence of a moral quality was, as such, a prepotent

§ 4 · MAN'S APTITUDE FOR VIRTUE

reason for a certain line of conduct. But with the help of our present definition of a moral judgement an alternative account might be attempted. Let us divide moral qualities into positive and negative – those whose inherence in an action or an end would be a reason for that action or for the pursuit of that end, and those which would constitute a reason *against*. If it is the case that a certain end is good or a certain action is obligatory, we may speak of that state of things as a positive moral truth: and correspondingly there would be negative moral truths.

It is supposable that, whenever someone makes a moral judgement, he also apprehends a moral truth, positive or negative, and whenever he apprehends a moral truth he also makes a moral judgement. In that case, the inclination, favourable or unfavourable, which is involved in his moral judgement, constitutes a reason for, or against, the course of action with which the moral truth he apprehends is concerned. Whoever discerns an obligation on his own part, is also disposed to fulfil it: for the discernment of the obligation is inseparable from the distinctive inclination of the will which we are calling a moral judgement. In this way we can maintain that someone who recognises a positive moral truth always has a reason for, and someone who recognises a negative moral truth always has a reason against a certain course of action, without having to introduce a peculiar and unique kind of reason, as we did in ch. 3, § 4. Yet this analysis will not suffice to do justice to Butler's notion of "authority". For when conscience speaks, there is not merely *a* reason, but, as we expressed it before, a prepotent reason for the conduct which conscience prescribes. Since men do not always heed their consciences, this prepotency cannot lie in an inclination of the will which is stronger than all contrary inclinations: and it must presumably lie in the special nature of the moral truth which people recognise in an act of conscience.

Butler would no doubt have been content to admit a universal correlation between moral judgements and apprehensions of moral truths; but we can hardly follow him.

Butler would have had little hesitation in accepting Kant's dictum that "an erring conscience is a chimera", and, as we have seen, never seriously contemplated the evidence for diversity of conscience. He consequently did not use what, in ch. 3, § 5, we called the "Freudian" notion of conscience. Yet this notion is indispensable. We cannot deny that moral judgements are diverse. But if that is the case they cannot be perfectly correlated with apprehensions of moral truths. If there are some people in the world who judge hospitality to strangers favourably, and some who judge ferocity to strangers favourably – and we know that such divergences exist – both parties cannot be apprehending a moral truth about the conduct which is right towards strangers.

In Butler's view, human nature is adapted to virtue, but not to vice, in the sense that by leading a good life, and only by leading a good life, all the needs of men's nature can be satisfied, or at least the largest combination of them which is practicable. As was noticed in ch. 4, § 4, Butler passes uncritically from the proof that there are instances of good men being happy and wicked men miserable to the universal conclusion that, not merely some men sometimes, but all men always consult their interests best by living virtuously. But he tacitly admits that the universal conclusion must rest on revelation, not experience, when he disposes of apparent exceptions with the remark that "all shall be set right at the final distribution of things".

The power of making moral judgements is, on this view, present in all men, either latently or actively. When it becomes active in any man it leads to the same results as it would in any other. When it is not only active but acted upon, it leads to the satisfying of a man's whole nature, or at least to the best possible approximation to such satisfaction. But what, then, of the potential opposition between moral judgements and self-love, which in § 3 we made part of our definition of a moral judgement, and claimed that Butler would accept as part of the notion of conscience?

It is clear that Butler must accept the distinctness of con-

§ 4 · MAN'S APTITUDE FOR VIRTUE

science and self-love. But it is more difficult to say just where he stands on the question of opposition between them. Presumably he would have to hold that their opposition is only a logical possibility, of which there are no actual instances.

But a difficulty arises here which has already been touched on. Full acceptance of the conclusion that human nature is satisfiable, and only satisfiable, by virtue depends on revelation. Butler has therefore not achieved, what he would certainly have wished, a presentation of man's aptitude for virtue which is equally acceptable to all, whatever their theological beliefs or disbeliefs. It may be that, as Butler would hold, through the love of God conscience and self-love are resolved into one another, and dialectical problems about the relation between the cognitive and affective parts of a moral judgement disappear or become trivial. But if the realisation of this truth is indispensable to our profiting by Butler's teaching, he is not offering us an autonomous ethical theory.

If we accept, on whatever grounds, Butler's view of the aptitude for virtue of human nature, there is a further difficult problem for anyone who regards the human race as subject to evolution. For it must be supposed that there have been earlier phases in human history in which the satisfactions and frustrations of which human beings were capable were very different from what they are now. Then, if morality is immutable, and if human nature as it is now is adapted to virtue, there may well have been other times at which human nature was not so adapted. The easiest solution would perhaps be to argue that, as was pointed out in ch. 3, § 1, the immutability of morality does not imply that identical moral rules are to be followed in dissimilar situations. In an earlier phase of human development, in the Stone Age perhaps, human needs and passions were in some respects different from what they are now. It follows that in their dealings with one another men at that time were commonly faced with situations unlike those with which we are commonly faced now. In that case it is supposable that, from the very same moral principles,

[181]

a course of conduct might follow different from that which is right for us to-day; and that the different human nature of those ages might be just as well adapted to be happy in that course of conduct as ours is to be happy in the conduct which is right for us.

§ 5 · *The general questions of ethical theory*

It was proposed in § 3 that moral philosophers should regard moral judgements, in our special Pickwickian sense, as the common subject-matter of their theories, and should formulate the points about which they differ as questions about the further characteristics of moral judgements, beyond those implied in their definition. What sort of questions would they be?

In the first place, moral philosophers have been much concerned with attempts to justify moral judgements, or certify them, or give some proof or assurance that they are to be relied on. Now this kind of attempt seems very much like the attempts which have been made, in other connections, to justify this or that kind of *belief*. Suppose I judge, as many people do, that, with certain exceptions, lying is wrong. My making of this judgement includes my being unfavourably disposed towards actual and possible acts of lying, no matter by whom performed, or in what circumstances – apart from the recognised exceptions; and my being so disposed even in cases in which it might suit me to tell a lie. Similarly, my believing that the weather is colder in winter than in summer includes my being disposed to put on warmer or cooler clothes as the seasons change, to lay in stocks of coal, to be surprised if the thermometer reads 80 degrees in January, or snow falls in July, and to be unsurprised by the contrary happenings. My belief is justified if my management of clothes and heating is, on the whole, successful, if surprises are rare, and absences of surprise frequent. But although it is relatively easy to satisfy ourselves that such a belief has, as regards the past,

§ 5 · GENERAL QUESTIONS

been justified by its success in the past, philosophers have often thought that it is difficult, or even impossible, to use past success as a justification for extending my belief to the future. Now what is being sought here seems to be a superior kind of proof, or a superior kind of evidence, or a superior analysis of the evidence, which will show that, in spite of an appearance to the contrary, past experience is, and will continue to be, a reliable guide to the future.

But the justification which might be demanded for a moral judgement seems to be of a different order. For it seems hardly intelligible to speak of a moral judgement as successful or unsuccessful: at most, we might speak of it in those terms according to a man's success or lack of success in bringing about actions of the approved kind and minimising actions of the condemned kind. But success or failure of that kind depends, not on the subject of the moral judgement, not, that is, on the acts favoured or condemned; but on the character and circumstances of the maker of the judgement. The only thing that will satisfy us, as a vindication of the moral judgement, will be some assurance related to the nature and effects of lying, and independent of the success or failure of individuals in avoiding and discouraging the telling of lies. We wish to be assured that *anyone* who condemns lying does well to do so.

This suggests that what we are seeking is a secondary moral judgement, directed not towards actions, but towards people's moral attitudes to actions. And to make secondary moral judgements is, as a matter of fact, a common practice. For example, we often condemn a censorious temper. But secondary moral judgements surely cannot give us the required assurance: for whatever doubt or uncertainty may attach to primary moral judgements must attach also to them, as it would to tertiary moral judgements, and so on for ever. By such a method we could never reach an assessment or certification of moral judgements: we should only be piling up moral judgements one upon another. If a primary moral judgement needs to be in some way reinforced, it must be reinforced by something of a different nature. If the earth would fall, did it not rest upon the back of an elephant, and the elephant upon a tortoise, the tortoise also needs support.

In fact moralists have seldom, if ever, avowedly pursued this method. What next suggests itself, and what has recommended itself to many moral philosophers, is the supposition that, over and above people's approvals and disapprovals, there are certain qualities – 'moral' qualities – which may belong to actions or to ends, and which stand in a very special relation to attitudes of approval or disapproval. But this special relation is hard to define. Let us use the words 'right' and 'wrong', for the moment, to stand for those qualities, whatever their nature may be, on whose presence or absence the warrantability of moral judgements is to depend.

Since, in spite of Butler, we must assume diversity of conscience, people will sometimes make moral judgements in favour of actions which are – what we are now calling – right, and sometimes against them. People's moral judgements will be mistaken or unwarranted when they approve of what is wrong or disapprove of what is right, and correct or justified when they approve of what is right and disapprove of what is wrong. But what is the relation between rightness and approval, and between wrongness and disapproval, in virtue of which rightness *justifies* approval? There is only one easy answer, and it has been tacitly assumed by many moral philosophers.

The easy answer is that moral judgements are not merely moral dispositions, but contain within themselves something cognitive or intellectual; namely a sense of, or belief in, or perception of, a relation between a moral quality and some real or imagined action or end. In that case a moral judgement is justified when an action supposed to be right or wrong actually is right or wrong, and unjustified in the contrary case. In short, sound and unsound moral judgements are merely a special case of knowledge and error, or true and false opinion, or perception and misperception. We find this cognitive model so profoundly satisfying, and it seems so

§ 5 · GENERAL QUESTIONS

obvious to us that those who differ from us on moral questions are in a state of intellectual unenlightenment, that the applicability of the model has seldom been questioned.

Yet this account of the way in which a moral judgement may be warranted or unwarranted generates a problem just as grave as that which it is supposed to solve. We obtain an intelligible relation between moral judgements and moral truths only at the expense of transferring the lacuna to a place inside the moral judgement itself; as when by buttoning a tight garment at one point we burst a seam elsewhere. For a moral judgement must now contain two elements; in the first place a disposition or attitude, a universalisable tendency to favour or condemn, and secondly a cognitive state, perception of or belief about the possessing of a moral quality by an end or action. And the relation between these two parts of a moral judgement reproduces the obscurity which we previously noticed about the relation between rightness and approval. In its earlier form this puzzle might be expressed in the question 'why is it appropriate to be favourably disposed towards what is right, but not towards what is wrong?': in its later form it might be expressed in the form 'why is it appropriate to be favourably disposed towards what *I see* to be right, or what *I believe* to be right . . . ?'.

This enigma has not always appeared in the foreground of ethical writings, because moralists have often treated moral judgements as being merely judgements in the ordinary cognitive sense – acceptances of propositions or recognitions of facts – and nothing more. Yet probably few moral philosophers would deny that there must be something more, once the question was raised. For it is very paradoxical to suppose that a man might recognise, let us say, the truth that lying is wrong, and yet not be disposed to condemn lying in himself and others, and feel no prickings of conscience on telling a lie. It is perfectly supposable that he should recognise the moral truth, and yet constantly tell lies himself, and connive at the lies of others: but not that he should do so with entire serenity. If he tells lies, or promotes lying, he must be inwardly self-condemned. And if he is not, if he tells lies without suffering the smallest interior struggle, it becomes incredible that he really accepts the proposition that lying is wrong. We say that he pays lip service to it, but no more; either from hypocrisy, or because he repeats moral apophthegms by rote without ever having reflected on their meaning.

(This line of argument lends support, incidentally, to our definition of 'moral judgement'. For it has been shown that a moral disposition is indispensable to the existence of what, according to established usage, is to be called a moral judgement: and there does not seem to be any equally cogent means of showing that some sort of recognition of moral qualities is indispensable.)

It is this mysterious bond, which appears to hold between a moral disposition and the recognition of a moral truth, to which Butler refers when he speaks of the "authority" of conscience, and of which an alternative description was given when we introduced the notion of 'intrinsic stringency' (ch. 3, §§ 4, 5). And it was no doubt Butler's sense of the strength of this bond which led him to choose those pregnant phrases, "sentiment of the understanding", and "perception of the heart", which were commented on in ch. 3, § 2.

But we have not done much to explain the nature of the bond by giving it a name. By choosing a name with suitable associations we may help to produce insight into the bond's nature. But if that is the best we can do, the question whether this bond exists, and if so how it is to be conceived, is taken out of the sphere of discussion. As we saw in ch. 3, § 5 it is arguable that the whole of what we express, when we use such words as 'right' or 'good', consists of some reference to our feelings, or attitudes, or dispositions to praise and blame. On this view, the whole notion of moral qualities, and of a distinct class of moral truths which contain moral qualities among their terms, is chimerical. And consequently there is no such thing as the apprehension of a moral truth, or the entertaining of a proposition about moral qualities. There cannot therefore be any bond between moral dispositions and

§ 5 · GENERAL QUESTIONS

apprehensions of moral truths, and any question as to the kind of suitability which holds between approval and recognition of rightness, or condemnation and recognition of wrongness, is confused or senseless.

Let us refer to this line of thought as the 'attitude' theory. According to the attitude theory, there can be no such process as justifying or authenticating a moral judgement. For as we have already seen, the only justifying process available would be the making of a secondary moral judgement; and that in its turn would stand in the same need of justification – if there were such a need – as the primary moral judgement it was supposed to justify.

But if we reject the attitude theory, we must at some point or other admit a suitability between value and conduct, or between attitudes and moral truths, about which nothing can be said beyond noting its existence and giving it a name. If what we mean when we speak of the wrongness of lying does not consist simply of people's dispositions to condemn lying, it must include some other characteristic, which might or might not belong to lying, and which might or might not belong to any end or action which people condemn or approve of. That other characteristic, when perceived, may *in fact* evoke condemnation or approval of what possesses it. But so may any characteristic whatever – according as it matches people's interests and desires, or fails to do so. Because a man loves money, or praise, or power, we do not say that there is a necessary and unanalysable connection between those objects and his attitudes in relation to them: whatever connection there may be arises from the natural history of his character and temperament, the causes which made him the man he is. But we are not satisfied with that kind of contingent connection between moral qualities and the attitudes they evoke – we are not satisfied that the relation should be merely one of the brute facts we find out by experience.

For people of a moralising bent, it is difficult to resist the assumption that those who are morally astray are in error in just the same fashion as those who are mistaken about

[187]

questions of fact or theory; and conversely that there is such a thing as moral wisdom, which is veracious and reliable in the same style as are accurate observations and well supported theories. When this assumption is strongly held, any form of attitude theory must be unacceptable. If we survey the ills and miseries that men inflict upon one another, we wish to think that their conduct would be different if they rightly understood what they were doing. It is often supposable that bad conduct comes from mistakes on matters of fact – that, as Butler sometimes urges, if men were less blind to their own interests, and steadier in the pursuit of relatively remote gains, the harm they do would be much abated. But making every allowance for the good results which good luck or a kind Providence might draw from self-interest, once adequately enlightened, we cannot feel sure that that enlightenment would suffice to produce universal good conduct: while we feel quite sure that right is right and wrong is wrong, and that something is amiss with those who do not know the difference. It follows that we cannot admit that what is amiss with them is merely a mistake about matters of fact: for, if we thought that, we should be quite sure, and not merely, at best, hopeful, that enlightened self-interest was a moral panacea.

If we are willing to pursue this train of thought, and to reject attitude theories, we can hardly avoid reaching some position akin to Butler's. There must be moral qualities, which human actions or their results may possess or lack. The presence or absence of a moral quality depends on the intrinsic nature of those actions or results: if an action is good, any other similar action, at any place or time, must be good, unless the latter, or some effect of it, or some whole to which it belongs, differs in some morally relevant way from the former. We have some power of knowing the moral qualities of things and actions. There is a distinctive relation of fittingness, or 'intrinsic stringency', between moral qualities and conduct, in virtue of which actions and moral judgements may conform or fail to conform to moral truths. The nature of this relation may be felt, but cannot be analysed. When we

§ 5 · GENERAL QUESTIONS

discern a moral truth relevant to our own conduct, we not only see that our conduct may conform or fail to conform to it, but feel its claim upon us: without this feeling of a claim on us we cannot properly be said to discern the truth in question at all. The word 'claim' here does not introduce a new idea, or an analysis of the distinctive moral relation. It is a synonym for what Butler called "authority". The best we can do to express the distinctive moral relation is to ring the changes upon suggestive names for it — 'authority', 'stringency', 'claim', 'requirement', and so on. We have seen that Butler at times, with a preacher's innocent lack of scruple, goes a considerable way towards admitting that this claim is nothing more than the claim of interest and prudence. For he was often willing to beguile his worldly auditors to be better men than they would choose to be thought: in one of his charity sermons, he remarks that "since the generality will not part with their vices, it were greatly to be wished they would bethink themselves, and do what good they are able, so far only as is consistent with them" (*sc.* with their vices — *S.P.* 2.10). But it has been shown that, if Butler's whole intention was to recommend virtue on prudential grounds, his distinction between conscience and self-love, his careful introduction of the concept of authority and supremacy, and his recognition of an eternal immutable morality, would all be mere aberrations.

INDEX

See also titles of sections in the table of contents. References to Butler's writings, and quotations from them, are too numerous to be indexed.

Affections, *see* Passions
Appetites, *see* Passions
Aristotle, 82
Attitudes, and attitude theories, 90–1, 187
  universalisable, 170–8, 184–7
Authority, *see* Conscience

Bartlett, Rev. Thomas, his *Life* of B., 15, 24, 40
Beerbohm, Sir Max, 82
Benevolence, 45–6, 57–9
  how related to self-love, ch. 4 §4
  pleasant to its possessor, 63, 65–6
  whether the whole of virtue, ch. 5 §2
Benson, Bp. Martin, 26
Bentham, Jeremy, 120
Berkeley, Bp. George, 39–40
Blackburne, Abp. Lancelot, 17
Broad, C. D., 11, 49, 57–9
Byrom, Dr John, 18–19

Caroline, Queen, 17–19, 26
Causation, ch. 6 §2
Chapman, Dr Thomas, 23–4
Clarke, Dr Samuel, 16, 35–6
Conscience, authority of, ch. 2 §2; ch. 3; 160, 186

Conscience – *continued*
  'Freudian' and 'Kantian', 92–4, 176, 180
  meaning of the word for B., ch. 3 §1
  uniformity and diversity of, ch. 3 §§1 and 6; 166, 180, 184
Cumberland, Duke of, 18

Deists, 35
Desert, ch. 6
Determinism, ch. 6 §3
Disinterestedness, ch. 4 §2

Egoism, whether advocated by B., ch. 4 §5: *see also* Psychological egoism
Evolution, of human nature, 181–2
  of moral codes, 72, 91–2
  of moral insight, 93–4

Final causes, ch. 7 §2: *see also* 'Objectives'
Forster, Dr Nathaniel, 25
Freedom of will, B. on, 36; ch. 6

George II, King, 18, 22
'Goals', of attitudes, 170–3 (not the same as 'objectives' of passions)

[190]

INDEX

God, in B.'s ethics, ch. 7; 181
  ethical concepts not definable in terms of, 142–3, 146–7
Goodness, of God, 142
  of human nature, ch. 7 § 3

Habits, 38–9
Hobbes, Thomas, 18, 64, 95, 99
  B.'s criticism of, ch. 4 § 3
  his doctrines alluded to, 32
Hume, David, 135
Hypnotism, vulgar notion of, 96–7

Ignorance, man's, 33–4, 150–1
Interest, *see* Self-love
"Interested action", meaning of, ch. 4 § 2
'Intrinsic stringency' of moral qualities, ch. 3 §§ 4–5; 178, 186, 188

James, William, 81, 100
Justice, 145, 156: *see also* Desert

Kant, Immanuel, 92

Language, B. on use of, ch. 1 § 2
  characteristic ethical, 120–2
Locke, John, 31, 37
Love, between persons, 152–3
  of God, ch. 7 § 4
  of what is good, 151–2, 155–8

Mahomet, 19
Men of the world, 40, 46, 63, 65, 113 ("men of pleasure"), 155, 189
Method, 66–7, 110
Moral dispositions, 176–7, 184–7: *see also* Attitudes

Moral judgements, ch. 8 § 3
  justification of, ch. 8 § 5
Moral law, 164–6
Motives, 108, 151

Naturalism and non-naturalism, ch. 8 § 2; 167–9
Nature, hierarchy in human, 43–4; ch. 2 § 2
  meaning of the word for B., ch. 2 § 1
Negligence, 137–9
Newcastle, Duke of, 22–4

'Objectives', of passions, ch. 2 § 3
  of actions, ch. 4 § 1
  differ in importance, 107
  ultimate subultimate and subordinate, 103, 106–7
Obligation, 143–4; ch. 8 § 1; 179
  and interest, 154–5
  conflicting o.'s, 161–2
  feeling of, 163
  moral and non-moral, 163–6
  "*prima facie*", 162
Oblomov, 39
Oriel College, Oxford, 16, 27

Passions, 43, 45–8, 98
  how related to self-love, ch. 2 § 4
  none inherently bad, ch. 7 § 3
  'occurrent' and 'continuant', 54–5, 57
  "public" and "private", 106
  strength of, 79–82
  their objects and 'objectives', ch. 2 § 3; 152–3
Personal identity, B. on, 36–8
Pleasure and pain, 50–1, 60, 98–100

[191]

INDEX

Psychological egoism, 32, 63–4; ch. 4 §§ 1 and 3

Reasons, for actions, ch. 3 §3; 114
   prepotent, 77, 83–4, 86, 160, 178–9
Reflection, *see* Conscience
Resentment, 149–50
Rolls Chapel, 17
Ross, Sir David, 162
Rules of morality, ch. 5

Secker, Abp. Thomas, 16, 17, 28
Self-deception, 96, 125, 172–3
Self-love, 45–8
   how related to benevolence, ch. 4 §4
   how related to conscience and virtue, 47; ch. 2 §5; 84–5, 115, 154–5, 180–1, 188–9
   how related to passions, ch. 2 §4
   its coincidence with conscience not proved empirically, 155, 180
   "supposed" and "immoderate", 59–60, 64, 85
Self-partiality, 64–5, 178
Stevenson, C. L., 90
Sympathy, 33, 109, 111–12

Talbot, Charles, Lord T., Lord Chancellor, 17, 18
Talbot, Rev. Edward, 16
Talbot, Bp. William, 16–17, 28
Talkativeness, B. on, 29
Teleology, *see* 'Objectives'
Treachery, 118–19, 121–4
Tribal moralities, 173–4
Truth and falsity, whether they belong to moral principles and judgements, 71–2, 175–180, 184–9
Tucker, Dr Josiah, 21

Unconscious aims, 53
Uniformity, of conscience and of duty, ch. 3 §§ 1 and 6
Uniformity, of human nature, assumed by B., 66
   of interest, 68; ch. 4 §2
Universalisability, *see* Attitudes
Utilitarianism, ch. 5 §2; ch. 6 §4
   objections to by B., ch. 5 §3

Value-bearing qualities, 75–7, 160–1

Walpole, Horace, 25
Walpole, Sir Robert, 19
Wesley, Rev. John, 18, 20–1